# W TO THE WORLD

W. OSCAR THOMPSON JR.,
CAROLYN THOMPSON RITZMANN,
*and* CLAUDE KING

LifeWay Press®
Nashville, Tennessee

Published by LifeWay Press®
© 2008 Claude King and Carolyn Thompson Ritzmann

The primary text for this study was adapted from *Concentric Circles of Concern:
Seven Stages for Making Disciples* by W. Oscar Thompson Jr. with Carolyn Thompson Ritzmann,
revised and updated by Claude King (Nashville: Broadman & Holman Publishers, 1999).

ISBN 978-1-4158-6272-8
Item 005085767

Dewey decimal classification: 248.5
Subject heading: WITNESSING \ EVANGELISTIC WORK \ DISCIPLESHIP

This book is a resource for course CG-1258 in the subject areas Evangelism
and Discipleship in the Christian Growth Study Plan.

Cover illustration: Mac Premo

To order additional copies of this resource, write to LifeWay Church Resources
Customer Service; One LifeWay Plaza; Nashville, TN 37234-0113; fax (615) 251-5933;
phone toll free (800) 458-2772; order online at *www.lifeway.com;*
e-mail *orderentry@lifeway.com;* or visit the LifeWay Christian Store serving you.

*Printed in the United States of America*

Leadership and Adult Publishing
LifeWay Church Resources
One LifeWay Plaza
Nashville, TN 37234-0175

# Contents

## Introducing
## *W. Oscar Thompson Jr., Carolyn Thompson Ritzmann, and Claude King*

1935–1980

**W. Oscar Thompson Jr.** was a pastor for 20 years before joining the faculty of Southwestern Baptist Theological Seminary in the area of evangelism. He served as the president of the Oscar Thompson Evangelistic Association; as a pastoral consultant for the Cancer Counseling and Research Foundation; and as a pastoral consultant and board member of the Trinity Valley Hospice Association, Incorporated. Thompson died of cancer in 1980 before developing a manuscript for *Concentric Circles of Concern*. That task was left to his widow Carolyn.

**Carolyn Thompson Ritzmann** is living what she believes is important in life: building and maintaining relationships. Carolyn was the wife and ministry partner of the late Oscar Thompson. After his death Carolyn edited his notes and transcripts of audiotapes to create the best-selling book *Concentric Circles of Concern*. Over the past 27 years Carolyn has been active in speaking and teaching on the subject of relationships, while taking on the additional challenge of relationships in a blended family by her marriage to widower Bud Ritzmann. Carolyn and Bud reside on a ranch in central Texas and are active in an intentional interim ministry to churches. They have three adult children and five grandchildren.

**Claude King** is an editor in chief for leadership and adult undated resources at LifeWay Christian Resources. In 1999 he and Carolyn worked together to revise and expand *Concentric Circles of Concern* for Broadman & Holman Publishers. Other LifeWay courses he has written or coauthored include *Experiencing God, Fresh Encounter, Come to the Lord's Table, The Mind of Christ, The Call to Follow Christ, Pray in Faith,* and *Made to Count Life Planner*. He is married to Reta and has two daughters and one grandson.

*Note: The primary text in each daily lesson is written from the perspective of author Oscar Thompson.*

# Introduction

Prior to attending seminary in New Orleans, I served on the church staff of a dynamic, evangelistic church in Nashville, Tennessee. I was trained in an evangelistic method that normally took our team to share the gospel with total strangers. However, we were prepared to break the ice and establish a relationship before talking about a person's spiritual needs. I am very grateful for that training experience because I studied the Scriptures and came to better understand what faith in Christ means. I learned how to use God's Word to tell others about His conditions for their salvation.

After going through the training course several times, I led the course for a while. From that perspective I made some observations. Although we saw a number of people pray to receive Christ in their homes, very few ever followed through with a public commitment to Christ. We were not very effective at helping these people get established in a local body of Christ where they could grow.

Many adults did make public professions of their faith in Christ, but most of these did not come directly from our evangelistic-visitation program. I noticed that most of these people were family members, relatives, neighbors, or friends of our members. God was using people who had learned to share the gospel with others to lead people in their circles of influence to Christ. These were the people we were able to effectively assimilate into the church.

We didn't really plan for this type of outreach. It happened only as God's people shared the gospel with those to whom they were related. Our planned evangelism strategy served primarily to prepare and equip people for sharing Christ. God took them from that point and used them to share through their relationships. During this time I felt uneasy about the fact that our greatest evangelist fruit came not from our evangelistic program but through unplanned experiences of our members.

While I was attending seminary in the early 1980s, I came across *Concentric Circles of Concern* in the bookstore. As I began to read the experiences of Oscar and Carolyn Thompson, I kept thinking, *This is it!* Concentric circles explained what God had done through relationships in my previous church. I began to wonder why this book was not required reading for every seminary student. It explained in moving ways how I could guide God's people to share Christ in a very natural way with the people they knew and loved. I saw the way I could help people be used by God to show His love and see loved ones drawn to Jesus. If every believer reached his or her concentric circles, the whole world could be drawn to Christ.

When I began to develop and write curriculum for lay discipleship, I saw two types of books. One was very inspiring and informative, but I could read it and never change over time. It was like preaching an evangelistic message without giving an invitation to respond.

The other type called me to apply what I was learning. Then in a small-group context other Christians could help me follow through in the application in ways that thoroughly changed my life. As I watched what God did through courses like *Experiencing God, Fresh Encounter,* and *The Mind of Christ,* I developed a conviction that book writers should regularly give an invitation for a reader to respond and apply the truths being taught.

In 1999 I revised *Concentric Circles of Concern* to do just that. The message has so impacted my own life that I sensed God would use it in even greater ways as Christians helped one another make the applications to their own lives and ministries.

When I returned to LifeWay in 2005, we began developing the Growing Disciples Series, designed to teach new and growing disciples how to follow Christ as they learn and practice six foundational Christian disciplines. To teach the discipline of witness to the world, I could think of no more effective approach than the one presented in *Concentric Circles of Concerns.* By reaching out with God's love to those in your ever-widening circles of influence, you can witness to your world for Christ.

As a result of this study, you will be able to—
- explain how the gospel spreads through relationships;
- evaluate your vertical relationship with God and your horizontal relationships with others in order to be reconciled in all of your relationships;
- identify immediate-family members, relatives, friends, neighbors, associates, and acquaintances in your circles of influence who need to know and trust Jesus Christ as Savior and Lord;
- complete survey forms that help you identify the needs of lost people in your concentric circles and ways you can meet those needs;
- intercede in prayer for those who are yet to believe in Jesus Christ;
- build relational bridges and show God's love to people who are yet to believe;
- prepare yourself to introduce people to Jesus Christ;
- identify ways to become involved in God's worldwide redemptive mission.

## SMALL-GROUP STUDY OF *WITNESS TO THE WORLD*

Although you could study this book alone, I want you to experience God's best. When God saved you, He placed you in the body of Christ so that you can benefit from the ministry of other members of the body. You are also in the body to help others. The writers of Hebrews instructed us, "Let us be concerned about one another in order to promote love and good works, not staying away from our meetings, as some habitually do, but encouraging each other" (Heb. 10:24-25). I encourage you to join a group of other believers in Christ and work through this study together. You will find that we need one another, and we can help one another live the truths of this study.

If you are the person who will lead the small-group sessions, you will find a brief leader guide on pages 80–88. For each of the six sessions, we've suggested learning activities that will guide you to share, process, and apply what you are learning.

## PERSONAL STUDY OF *WITNESS TO THE WORLD*

This book is designed for you not simply to read but to actually interact with the concepts you study. We've given you several types of activities to help you respond to the Lord as He teaches you how to share His love with others.

*Five daily lessons.* Each week you will study five daily lessons before meeting with a small group to process what you are learning. Don't wait until the end of the week to start your study. Set aside time to spend with the Lord each day for working on the study. This will help you develop a daily time to come before the Lord and allow Him to encounter you. For the next six weeks let this book be your guide for your daily time with the Lord. By starting the day with your focus on Christ, His Word, and His work, you will be in a position all day to let God apply biblical truths to your life. As you do this one day at a time, you will learn and grow at a reasonable pace. *You will need to study week 1 before your first small-group session.*

*Prayer.* Several prayer activities are included in the study. At the end of your personal study each day, you will find an activity called "Praying for My Circles Today." By praying as suggested, you will utilize prayer as a significant strategy for reaching people in your circles of influence. Other prayer activities are found in the text. They are indicated by an arrow pointing up to God and down to you, symbolizing the way prayer is to function. Prayer is communication with God that goes both ways: you talk to the Lord, and He speaks to you. Please do not omit or rush through these times of prayer, but stop and spend time with the Lord. These may very well be life-changing moments between you and the Lord.

*Personal response.* Another type of activity, indicated by an orange, circled number, tests your understanding of the previous text, helps you make application to your own life, or gives another assignment for you to accomplish. Several activities will direct you to complete portions of the Discipleship Helps at the back of the book. These activities will help you identify the people in your life who are yet to believe in Jesus Christ and apply the principles in this study to meet their needs and point them to Christ.

By completing these activities as you read, you will get the most from your study. God wants to use you to reach others through the relationships in your life. Make yourself available to Him, and you will be surprised by what He will do through you.

Claude King

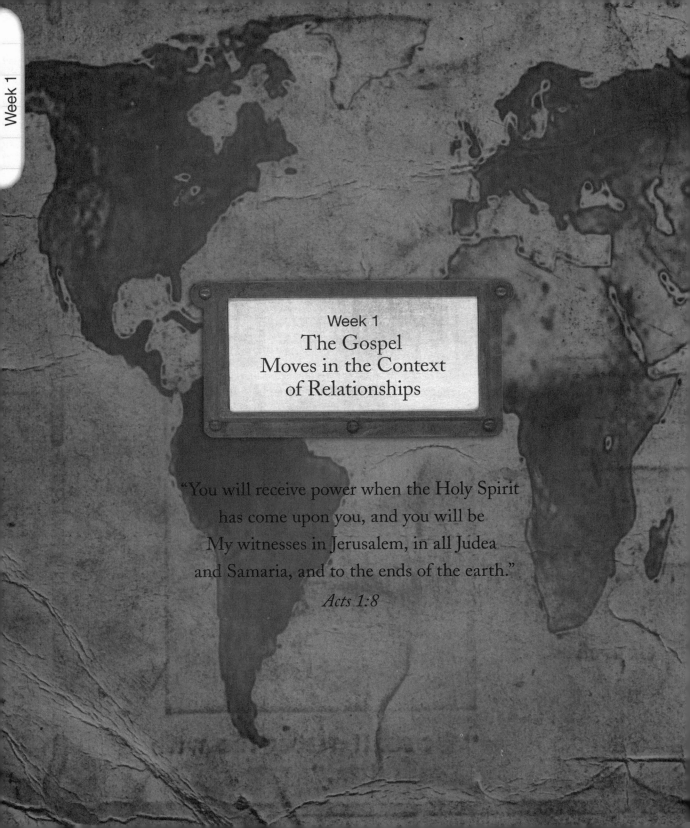

Week 1

# The Gospel
# Moves in the Context
# of Relationships

"You will receive power when the Holy Spirit
has come upon you, and you will be
My witnesses in Jerusalem, in all Judea
and Samaria, and to the ends of the earth."

*Acts 1:8*

For 24 years I preached and pastored churches. Most of the concepts of evangelism I had read stressed training believers to tell people they had not previously met about the Lord. I call a stranger like this Person X.

A person can never lead another closer to the Lord than he or she already is. Evangelism must flow from a life that is deeply in love with the Lord. It is not something you can learn in a textbook, take tests on, and be assured of success. When you get out into the world, if you do not have a godly lifestyle, you will flunk the course. Your lifestyle should reveal who you really are.

Some men are able evangelists in the pulpit and have led many people to make decisions for the Lord in their services. Yet I have watched these same men act rudely toward a waitress or a salesperson and be first-class, worldly Christians. There is no excuse for this behavior. What does the world see in your daily life? Does the world see Jesus?

The essence of a walk in Jesus Christ is His desire to produce His character within a Christian. If you are a Christian, you have a ministry, and that ministry is to reach the world around you for Jesus Christ. God wants you to express that ministry wherever you are. He wants to love your world through you and to draw it to Him. If you let barriers hinder you from doing this, little else you accomplish in life matters, for your basic purpose in life will go unfulfilled. Your life will be desperately empty.

## OVERVIEW OF WEEK 1
Day 1: The New Testament Pattern of Evangelism
Day 2: Reconciled at Home
Day 3: New Testament Relationships
Day 4: Spheres of Influence
Day 5: Reconciled with an Absentee Father

## VERSE TO MEMORIZE
"You will receive power when the Holy Spirit has come upon you, and you will be My witnesses in Jerusalem, in all Judea and Samaria, and to the ends of the earth" (Acts 1:8).

## DISCIPLESHIP HELPS FOR WEEK 1
Concentric Circles of Concern (p. 89)
Survey Forms: Circles 2–3 (pp. 90–93)
Praying for Those Yet to Believe (p. 101)
Preparing Your Story (pp. 102–3)

# *Day 1* • The New Testament Pattern of Evangelism

## God's Word for Today

"You will receive power when the Holy Spirit has come upon you, and you will be My witnesses in Jerusalem, in all Judea and Samaria, and to the ends of the earth" (Acts 1:8).

Read and meditate on "God's Word for Today" (this week's verse to memorize) in the margin and spend a moment in prayer as you begin today's lesson. Remove the Scripture-memory card from the back of your book and begin committing this verse to memory.

After recognizing the seriousness of the task before me in teaching evangelism to seminary students, I committed myself to read through the New Testament once a month, looking for evangelistic strategy. Every teacher and pastor always looks for fresh, new ways of doing things. You do not want to do everything the same old way. But you must do everything in a biblical way. How did the early Christians do evangelism in the New Testament?

As I studied the New Testament, I looked for a strategy, an idea. Finally, I began to see it rise like fog in the morning above a forest. At first it was almost imperceptible. Then all at once it became clear: the most important word in the English language is *relationship*.

1. **Read Acts 1:8 in the margin ("God's Word for Today") and complete the pattern described. We will be witnesses in—**

    1. _____
    2. _____
    3. _____
    4. _____

In the New Testament church the gospel always moved on lines of relationship—to Jerusalem, Judea, Samaria, the ends of the earth—and in waves that seemed to move outward. Have you ever thrown a rock in a pond and watched the waves move in all directions until they reached every edge of the pond? That was the pattern I saw. The gospel of Jesus Christ began to spread through relationships in ever-growing circles.

It seemed to me that we always trained people in evangelism to go to Person X out there somewhere—someone they have never met. But no prior relationship had been established with Person X. Lifestyle evangelism in the New Testament did not begin with Person X. It worked through relationships that had already been established.

After I had been teaching at the seminary awhile, I was asked to teach an evangelism class for a couple of nights for a friend at a Bible institute.

As I drove to class that first night, I mulled over this concept of relationship evangelism. When I got to class, I drew seven circles on the board to resemble a target with a bull's-eye in the center—concentric circles.

I said to the class, "The gospel moves on contiguous lines—on lines of relationship." I explained the circles and what each circle represented:

- Circle 1 is self.
- Circle 2 is immediate family.
- Circle 3 is relatives.
- Circle 4 is close friends.
- Circle 5 is neighbors and associates.
- Circle 6 is acquaintances.
- Circle 7 is Person X.

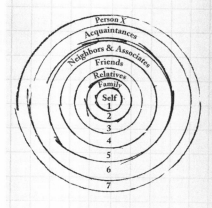

I explained that God holds us responsible for everyone He brings into our sphere of influence. Many of us would rather focus on circle 7 to salve our consciences, because we don't want to deal with ruptured relationships in circles 2–6.

When we have ruptured relationships horizontally with people, we also have a ruptured relationship vertically with God. Although we know the Lord, we are not willing to let Him be Lord of everything and accept, love, and forgive people on His conditions.

With Person X, on the other hand, our lifestyles do not have to be consistent. We can talk to Person X and then be on our way. There is nothing wrong with telling Person X about Jesus. We are supposed to do that. God brings these people into our lives. However, if we do not tell people in circles 2–6 about the Lord, we are hypocritical. If our relationship with the Lord is authentic, we want to share the good news of Christ with those closest to us as much as we do with strangers.

② **On the diagram on page 89, list persons in your concentric circles of concern. We'll work on a more detailed survey later. Begin by listing the names of one or two persons in each of the circles.**

③ **Look back over your list and circle the names of persons who do not know Jesus Christ as their personal Savior. If you don't know, write a question mark beside the name.**

**Pray as suggested in "Praying for My Circles Today."**

**Praying for My Circles Today**

Begin praying for the persons whose names you have listed on the diagram on page 89.

- Ask the Lord to show you any broken relationship that needs mending. If He reveals one, begin praying about how to be reconciled.
- Ask the Lord to make you a channel of His love to these persons.
- Ask the Lord to give you sensitivity to their needs.
- For those who do not know Jesus as their Savior, ask God to begin engineering circumstances in their lives to draw them to Himself.

## *Day 2* • Reconciled at Home

 Read and meditate on "God's Word for Today" in the margin
and spend a moment in prayer as you begin today's lesson.

### God's Word for Today

"The Lord appointed 70 others, and He sent them ahead of Him in pairs to every town and place where He Himself was about to go. He told them: "The harvest is abundant, but the workers are few. Therefore, pray to the Lord of the harvest to send out workers into His harvest. Now go; I'm sending you out like lambs among wolves" (Luke 10:1-3).

In day 1 I told you about a time when I filled in as the teacher for a friend's evangelism class. As I spoke to that class, I noticed a woman sitting on the back row. I watched her face distort. She was hurting. She was either having a gall-bladder attack, or I was saying something that was hurting her. It was the latter. She left very quickly that night, not knowing that she would have to put up with me again.

I came back the next week. She was not expecting me. She looked up and said, "Oh, you again!" That always warms a teacher's heart! She sat down and said, "I want to see you after class." Wow! I had not been talked to like that since the second grade.

After class the woman came to my desk and said, "You hurt me last week."

I said, "I don't understand."

"You said I came here to study to tell Person X about the Lord." She had personalized it. She had internalized it. She continued, "You see, I was estranged from my husband and my two sons. It was not their fault. It was mine. I came here to salve my conscience. Last week the Holy Spirit took hold of me. I knew I must go home."

As the woman wept, she said, "I want you to know that I have accepted Jesus Christ's conditions for reconciliation. You see, my conditions would never have reconciled us. I had to accept Jesus Christ's conditions."

Please understand this. You may accept another person's conditions, or you may go with your conditions to establish a relationship, but it will never be a lasting relationship until you accept Jesus Christ's conditions. Why? Because that is the way you are designed.

The woman continued, "I am back at home now. But do you know what has happened? The timidity I've always had toward Person X is gone. When Jesus became Lord of my relationships, He took away my timidity."

I said, "That's it—relationships!"

If there are ruptured relationships between you and those in your concentric circles, there will be a rupture of the flow of the Holy Spirit through your life. Jesus put it very plainly in Matthew 5:23-24.

1. Read Matthew 5:23-24 in the margin. Why do you think Jesus taught us to restore relationships before worshiping God?

_____

_____

**Matthew 5:23-24**
"If you are offering your gift on the altar, and there you remember that your brother has something against you, leave your gift there in front of the altar. First go and be reconciled with your brother, and then come and offer your gift."

Jesus taught us to confess wrong relationships and make them right before coming to worship the Father. We must be reconciled with others to be right with God.

I believe with all my heart that when you have to dig deep into your spiritual well to get the Living Water flowing, there is something wrong in a relationship somewhere. When relationships are right, the flow of the Holy Spirit is like an artesian well that bursts up and out and over! Evangelistic training will be less useful until we make those relationships right.

2. On page 90 make a list of the persons in your immediate family. On page 92 list those who are relatives by blood or marriage. Include the following persons, whether or not you know their spiritual condition.
   • Husband or wife
   • Mother and father
   • Stepparents
   • Your children
   • Stepchildren
   • Grandchildren
   • Sisters and brothers
   • Grandparents
   • Aunts and uncles (include great-)
   • Cousins
   • Nieces and nephews
   • In-laws (mother, father, sister, brother)

3. Read "Preparing Your Story" on page 102. Follow the directions to write your testimony so that you will be prepared to share Christ when opportunities arise.

 **Praying for My Circles Today**
Begin praying for your immediate-family members and relatives on a regular basis, especially those who are lost.

## Day 3 • New Testament Relationships

### God's Word for Today

"'My food is to do the will of Him who sent Me and to finish His work,' Jesus told them. 'Don't you say, "There are still four more months, then comes the harvest"? Listen to what I'm telling you: Open your eyes and look at the fields, for they are ready for harvest'" (John 4:34-35).

 Read and meditate on "God's Word for Today" in the margin and spend a moment in prayer as you begin today's lesson.

Accounts of relationships in the New Testament illustrate the natural way the good news can travel. At the beginning of Jesus' ministry, He began to choose disciples to follow Him. Andrew was the first.

 **Read John 1:35-42 in your Bible. What did Andrew do when he first met Jesus?**

_____

When Andrew met the Savior of the world—Jesus, the Messiah—his first instinct was to introduce his brother, Simon, (later named Peter) to Jesus. Though we don't read very much about Andrew, Peter became one of the great leaders of the early church and wrote two books of the New Testament. What a contribution Andrew made to the Kingdom! He carried the gospel of Jesus Christ to someone in his immediate family through a relationship.

Jesus found another disciple from the same hometown as Andrew and Peter.

 **Read John 1:43-51 in your Bible. What did Philip do when he met Jesus?**

_____

Philip met Jesus and responded to His invitation to follow Him. He then went to Nathanael and brought his friend to meet Jesus. When Nathanael met Jesus, he acknowledged that He must be the Son of God and the King of Israel. Many believe Nathanael is the same person who is called Bartholomew in the other three Gospels. These two friends became 2 of the 12 disciples Jesus chose to be His closest companions. Philip carried the good news about Jesus through a relationship to his friend, and both of their lives were changed forever.

Once Jesus took His disciples with Him on a journey through Samaria—a place most Jews avoided because of prejudice. Beside the well at a city named Sycar, Jesus introduced a woman to Himself as the Christ

(Messiah) and as the Living Water. She believed Him and immediately went to share the good news with her neighbors:

> The woman left her water jar, went into town, and told the men, "Come, see a man who told me everything I ever did! Could this be the Messiah?" They left the town and made their way to Him. …
>
> Many Samaritans from that town believed in Him because of what the woman said when she testified, "He told me everything I ever did." Therefore, when the Samaritans came to Him, they asked Him to stay with them, and He stayed there two days. Many more believed because of what He said. And they told the woman, "We no longer believe because of what you said, for we have heard for ourselves and know that this really is the Savior of the world" (John 4:28-30,39-42).

This woman was probably at the well at noon because she was not accepted by the other women who would normally draw water early in the day. She had been through five husbands and was living with a man she was not married to. When she realized Jesus was the long-awaited Messiah, she hurried back to town to share the good news with her neighbors and relatives. After only two days with Jesus, many believed in Him. One woman touched a whole city for Christ.

The New Testament gives other examples of people who carried the gospel through relationships to others:

- Paul described to the Ephesian elders how he had proclaimed the message of Christ "in public and from house to house" (Acts 20:20).
- When Cornelius (a Gentile) invited Peter (a Jew) to preach at his home, he invited all his household (probably including servants and family) to listen. These Gentiles believed Peter's message, and the Holy Spirit came down on them all (see Acts 10).
- Paul and Silas were in prison in Philippi singing hymns when an earthquake occurred. The jailer was ready to take his own life when Paul and Silas intervened. They told him and all in his house about Jesus. Before the night was over, the whole household believed in Christ and were baptized (see Acts 16:23-40).
- Jesus cast demons out of a wild man of the Gadarenes. Now in his right mind, the man was sent away and told by Jesus, " 'Go back to your home, and tell all that God has done for you.' And off he went, proclaiming throughout the town all that Jesus had done for him" (Luke 8:39).

**Praying for My Circles Today**

Pray about your willingness to share the gospel with people you come in contact with daily. Confess any reluctance or fear and ask God to give you courage and a willing heart. Commit to let Him use you to reach people in your circles of influence.

## Day 4 • Spheres of Influence

"The Son of Man has come to seek and to save the lost" (Luke 19:10).

"Jesus said to them again, 'Peace to you! As the Father has sent Me, I also send you'" (John 20:21).

Read and meditate on "God's Word for Today" in the margin and spend a moment in prayer as you begin today's lesson.

I went back to my own class at the seminary the next day after filling in for my friend at the Bible institute. My dear students never know what is going to happen next. I said, "Scratch everything; we're starting over." Because we were halfway through the semester, they looked at me the way a calf looks at a new gate.

I continued, "Class, I have a new assignment. It is an assignment you cannot finish this semester. You will not finish it until God takes you home."

I drew those concentric circles and explained that the gospel did not go from house to house to house to house down the street like a nice, neat census:

It went randomly from house to house to house to house on the path of relationships:

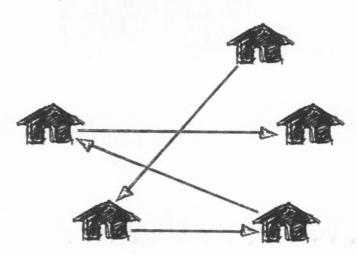

I continued, "God holds you responsible for every person who comes into your spheres of influence—into your concentric circles. You touch people in all of your circles every day, and you do not even see them. Some of them are cantankerous. Some of them you do not like, and some of them you really do not want to love. But they are there in relationship with you. They are there for you to love—to meet their needs—so that the Father can draw them to His Son, Jesus.

"How many of you have loved ones who you are not sure know the Lord? How many of you have come to seminary to learn only how to go and tell Person X about the Lord?" If you read the whole New Testament, you will see it. It is nothing profound, but it is as natural as anything can be. If something is genuine in my life and your life, we naturally want to share it with those we know.

1) **Can you think of a lost person whom God may have placed in your life for a reason? Write the person's name or initials.**

_____

2) **Turn to page 101. Read "Praying for Those Yet to Believe" and underline suggested ways to pray you want to use in praying for this person who is yet to believe in Christ.**

**Praying for My Circles Today**
Begin praying regularly for the person you identified at the end of today's lesson. Pray that God will open his or her heart to Jesus and will show you how to point him to Jesus through a loving relationship.

## Day 5 • Reconciled with an Absentee Father

### God's Word for Today

"God's chosen ones, holy and loved, put on heart-felt compassion, kindness, humility, gentleness, and patience, accepting one another and forgiving one another if anyone has a complaint against another. Just as the Lord has forgiven you, so also you must forgive. Above all, put on love— the perfect bond of unity" (Colossians 3:12-14).

**Matthew 6:14-15**

"If you forgive people their wrongdoing, your heavenly Father will forgive you as well. But if you don't forgive people, your Father will not forgive your wrongdoing."

⬍ Read and meditate on "God's Word for Today" in the margin and spend a moment in prayer as you begin today's lesson.

I had explained to my seminary class what the Lord had taught me about the concentric circles of relationship through which people shared the good news of Christ in the New Testament. Just as I was going to continue, a young man blurted out, "Dr. Thompson, I have all kinds of problems with that!" I turned and asked, "What's the matter, Jim?"

The impact of the moment had overwhelmed him. The assignment had touched an area of bitterness in his life that he did not know how to deal with. He said, "You don't understand! You grew up in a Christian home. But my father abandoned my mother and me 26½ years ago. I am 27 years old, and I have never seen him. I don't want to see him!"

I whispered, "Oh." A class of 60. He did not realize what had happened to him. All that pent-up anger just rolled out.

Gently, I turned to the board. Speaking silently to the Lord, I said, "Lord Jesus, love Jim through me. Please meet his need." A passage of Scripture came to mind. I wrote on the board Matthew 6:14-15. My translation was "Because of the love of Jesus and His forgiveness in my life, I must be ready to forgive if I am to be forgiven." I said, "In other words, you do not give people what they deserve. You give them what they need."

When I turned back around, the Holy Spirit was doing His work. I said, "Jim, I think you are in this class through divine providence. I think God is going to teach me something and you something and this class something. For if I cannot forgive another on the grounds of God's infinite grace, then God is going to have great difficulty forgiving me (see Matthew 6:14-15). Your father does not deserve forgiveness, but neither do you, and neither do I."

Tears were trickling down Jim's cheeks as the Holy Spirit descended on that class. Jim said, "What should I do? I don't know where my father is. He may not even be alive."

I said, "It doesn't matter. Take it to God, let Him tell you what to do, and leave it there. If God helps you find your father, you'll know what to do."

Jim said, "Yes."

We called the class to prayer.

1) Turn to the list of immediate-family members you recorded on page 90. Check the ones who have not yet placed their faith in Jesus Christ. Place a question mark if you aren't sure.

Weeks passed. One day Jim came sashaying into class about two feet off the ground. He said, "Dr. Thompson, I have something to say. I just have to share it. I can't wait!"

By that time I had lost my train of thought anyway, so I told him to go ahead. Jim said, "Last night I received two telephone calls. The first came from my mom saying that one of my godly aunts had gone to be with the Lord. I had always thought she was my mother's sister, but she wasn't. She was my father's sister who had stayed close to the family.

"At 11:00 I received a second call, and the voice on the other end said, 'Jim? Son? ... although I have no right to call you Son. I heard you are at Southwestern Seminary preparing for the ministry. I thought you would like to know that recently I gave my life to Jesus Christ. Can you forgive me for what I have done?'"

Jim said, "When I could quit sobbing, we talked. We spent an hour on the phone. My father said, 'Son, may I come to your graduation?'"

In May of that year we were marching in the processional of the graduation exercise in all our academic regalia when someone pulled me out of the line. It was Jim.

He took me over to a little man who looked up through his trifocals. In tears Jim said, "Dr. Thompson, this is my father. Dad, this is my professor."

What do you say? We went into a three-cornered hug. That is the gospel of Jesus Christ!

2) **If you have a family member who doesn't know the Lord, have you turned over this matter to God?** ○ Yes ○ No

3) **What is preventing reconciliation with your lost family member?**
○ Pride  ○ Time  ○ Money  ○ Reputation  ○ Comfort

Other: _____

_____

_____

_____

 **Praying for My Circles Today**
Pray about the lost family member you identified. Turn over his or her spiritual condition to God and express your willingness for God to use you to reach this person.

19

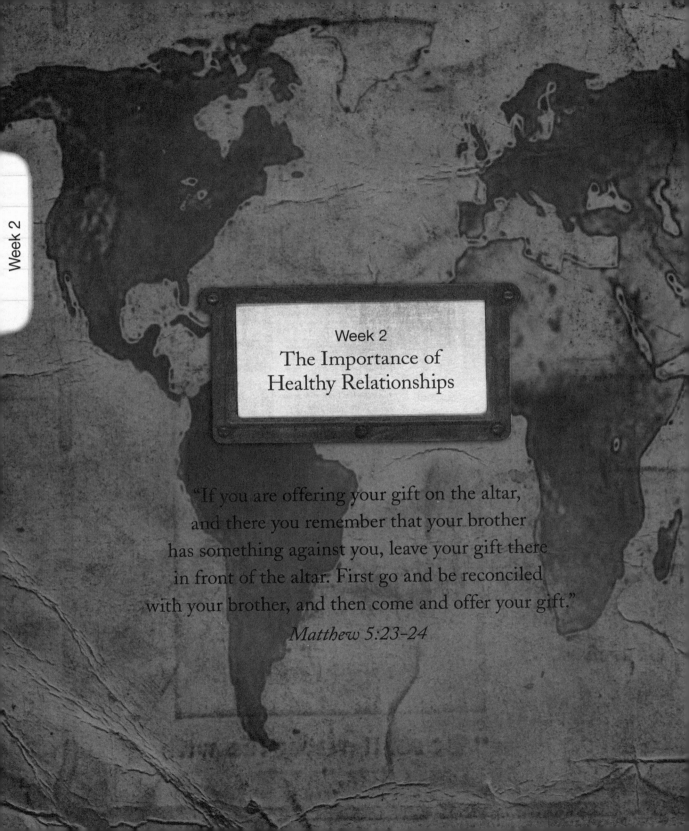

Week 2

# The Importance of Healthy Relationships

"If you are offering your gift on the altar,
and there you remember that your brother
has something against you, leave your gift there
in front of the altar. First go and be reconciled
with your brother, and then come and offer your gift."

*Matthew 5:23-24*

If your life is in turmoil today, I venture to say it's because of a ruptured relationship with someone. One purpose of this book is to explore what may be the causes of your broken relationships and to show how they can be mended so that you can reach out with God's love to those around you.

I want to help you experience restored relationships and begin to experience the best life has to offer. Right relationships will be a blessing not only to you but also to others around you. Your family will be blessed. Your friends, relatives, and coworkers will be blessed.

The key to a fulfilled life is relationships. Things do not satisfy; relationships do. The first relationship is with the Father. When He becomes the Lord of our lives, we forfeit forever the right to choose whom we will love. When He becomes Lord, He releases His love in us to build right relationships.

Through right relationships God's love can flow to bless all of the lives it touches. Will you allow God to use your life and your relationships as a channel for His love to flow to others?

## OVERVIEW OF WEEK 2

Day 1: A Lifelong Need
Day 2: Healthy Relationships
Day 3: Broken Relationships
Day 4: Restored Relationships
Day 5: A Channel of Love

## VERSE TO MEMORIZE

"If you are offering your gift on the altar, and there you remember that your brother has something against you, leave your gift there in front of the altar. First go and be reconciled with your brother, and then come and offer your gift" (Matthew 5:23-24).

## DISCIPLESHIP HELPS FOR WEEK 2

Survey Forms: Circle 2 (pp. 90–91)
Your Horizontal Relationships with Others (pp. 104–5)

## *Day 1* • A Lifelong Need

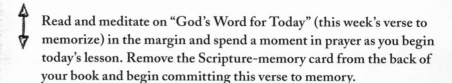

### God's Word for Today

"If you are offering your gift on the altar, and there you remember that your brother has something against you, leave your gift there in front of the altar. First go and be reconciled with your brother, and then come and offer your gift" (Matthew 5:23-24).

**Read and meditate on "God's Word for Today" (this week's verse to memorize) in the margin and spend a moment in prayer as you begin today's lesson. Remove the Scripture-memory card from the back of your book and begin committing this verse to memory.**

One December I boarded a plane bound for San Francisco and found my seat. On my right was a man who seemed very busy trying to get some writing done. He was a Hollywood producer. We greeted each other, but I did not bother him. After a time he put his pen down, and we began talking. He asked, "What do you do?" I long since have learned not to tell people I am a Baptist preacher, especially if I am on a three-hour flight. Instead I replied, "Well, I'm a teacher." Then I waited.

He asked, "What do you teach?" I wasn't about to tell him I teach evangelism at a theological seminary, so I said, "That's interesting you should ask. I basically teach that the most important word in the English language is *relationship*. If we can solve the relationship problems in this world, we will have solved domestic problems, neighbor problems, city problems, and international problems."

He looked out the window and thought for a moment, and then he said, "Hey, that's right!" Then I picked up a copy of *Time* and started reading. But he persisted, "Is that all you are going to tell me?"

"You want to know more?" So I explained that there are two types of relationships. There are horizontal relationships with people. Then there is the vertical relationship with the Creator of the universe, who has laid down the basis for all our other relationships. We are made by His design. If we follow His design, things work. If we do not follow His design, things do not work. Because man hasn't followed God's design, relationships are not working very well. Fortunately for us, however, God has also given us a plan to establish those right relationships. I told the man on the plane, "That plan is best seen in the teaching of Jesus Christ."

"Oh!" he said, "I've read the Bible. I agree with many things Jesus said. Now I don't believe everything the Bible says, but …"

"Well, that's what I teach." I went back to reading *Time* for a while and let him sort of hang there. "Tell me some more," the producer said.

To make a long story short, we talked for a long time during that flight. The man had many problems with the Scriptures. But many people in the secular world have rejected the Scriptures because they have heard only a caricature, not because they know anything about them. Similarly, most people have not rejected Jesus Christ but a caricature of Him. They have rejected "churchianity," but they haven't rejected Jesus Christ, because they have never really heard about Him. That is the tragedy. The producer and I talked about that. Then we talked about the person of Jesus Christ.

"How do you know who He is and what He is?" the man asked.

I responded that either Jesus was who He said He was, or He was psychotic, or He was a great fraud. "Dick," I said, "you are going to have to decide ultimately who He is on the basis of the evidence. You cannot just conclude that Jesus was the greatest teacher who ever lived. You see, this great teacher said, 'I am God.' And no great teacher is a falsifier. You are either going to have to take Jesus at His word or reject Him." Then I went back to reading *Time*.

I really began to pray, "Father, O Father, I cannot convince this fellow." He was having trouble in relationships with his workers and his family.

The latter part of that flight, I saw tears forming in his eyes as he looked out the window. Then he turned to me and said, "Oscar, this morning I got down on my knees in a motel room in Dallas. I prayed, 'Dear God, if there is a God, I have to have help. Please send somebody.'" He reached over and took me by my elbow and said, "God sent you. Now what do I do?"

"The first thing you have to do is surrender to the absolute authority of Jesus Christ and let Him be the Master of your life. You have to accept His conditions for coming to God. You cannot come on your own conditions.

"Dick, if you read the biography of every great Christian in history, you would find something very interesting. George Whitefield, John Wesley, Martin Luther, and many other great men of God intensely struggled in their search for God. All of them had one basic problem: though they were seeking God with all their hearts, they were seeking Him on their conditions. Only when they abandoned their conditions in coming to God did God accept them. When each one finally gave up and said, 'I will accept your conditions, whatever they are and whatever they cost me,' then instantly, immediately, God revealed Himself."

As Dick got off the plane, he looked over and said, "Thank you, Oscar. I have needed this all my life."

1) **Think about a lost person you know. What do you think he or she is refusing to give up to accept God's conditions for salvation?**
○ Pride   ○ Lifestyle   ○ Priorities   ○ Status   ○ Sin   ○ Pleasure
○ Assumptions   ○ Other: _____

**Praying for My Circles Today**

Spend time thanking God for the meaningful relationships in your life. If you had an unhappy home life, ask Him to help you heal. Ask Him to teach you how to develop healthy relationships through this study.

Remember to pray for the lost persons in your life and for your role in leading them to Christ.

## God's Word for Today

"I pray not only for these, but also for those who believe in Me through their message. May they all be one, as You, Father, are in Me and I am in You. May they also be one in Us, so the world may believe You sent Me. I have given them the glory You have given Me. May they be one as We are one. I am in them and You are in Me. May they be made completely one, so the world may know You have sent Me and have loved them as You have loved Me" (John 17:20-23).

# *Day 2* • Healthy Relationships

 **Read and meditate on "God's Word for Today" in the margin and spend a moment in prayer as you begin today's lesson.**

I believe the most important word in the English language, apart from proper nouns, is *relationship*. You may say, "But *love* has to be the most important word." I ask you, though, where is love going if there is no relationship? Relationship is the track. Love is what rolls over the track. Love moves through a relationship. But the thing that satisfies the deepest longing of your being is a relationship with someone.

You may think you want to be a Henry David Thoreau and go to a secluded Walden Pond to get away from the world. But Thoreau did not stay there forever, and neither could you. Why? There is something built into the nature of people that desires to be wanted, to be needed, to be fulfilled. Those desires are fulfilled only in relationships.

If we cannot get along with people, going off by ourselves may seem best. But we will not be fulfilled, because something in our nature cries out for fellowship. We have caused barriers in our relationships with others.

Rare is the individual who wants to be a loner. In being a loner, a person loses the purpose for existence, because God wants to reveal His character through a Christian's life. He does this by loving through you within relationships with others. John said, "What we have seen and heard we also declare to you, so that you may have fellowship along with us; and indeed our fellowship is with the Father and with His Son Jesus Christ" (1 John 1:3).

Consider warm, wonderful times of joy and happiness you have experienced. Do you remember—
- the warm caress of your parents' hands?
- the giggles and laughter as you romped with your friends or brothers and sisters in the bright sunshine of a summer afternoon?
- the ecstasy of your first date with that bright-eyed boy or girl?
- the joy or enthusiasm of those with whom you work?

1 **Identify two or three of the happiest experiences in your life and identify persons who were involved in those experiences with you.**

_____

_____

All of these relationships make you who you are. Right relationships with parents leave you mentally and emotionally ready for the new relationships of marriage and parenting. The special days of happiness—birthdays, anniversaries, Thanksgiving, Christmas—are fulfilling because of warm, wonderful relationships. Right relationships allow you to experience the best life has to offer.

The home is the basic institution in which God seeks to teach the sacredness of relationships and the skills for establishing and nourishing relationships. The home is the only institution designed to teach relationships. When this institution fails, a child is left mentally, emotionally, and spiritually crippled. To a large degree, the reason the world is coming unglued is because our best school for teaching relationships, the home, is not teaching correctly. If you solve relationship problems at home, you solve problems between husbands and wives, parents and children, brothers and sisters.

2️⃣ **List the top five most memorable or significant relationships you have ever had in your life.**

1. _____
2. _____
3. _____
4. _____
5. _____

It is likely that most of your most significant relationships have been with family members. The home is the context in which God places us to teach us how to have right relationships. The home under God should be the place to learn about relationships—husband and wife, parent and child, child and child. Here is where a person learns to love and to meet needs. A helpless baby who is placed in the hands of parents matures and develops the ability to love and to meet needs. A child is taught to submit his wayward, self-centered will to the will of the parents. Here selfishness, which is the root of sin, is replaced by the discipline needed to build relationships and to meet the needs of others.

God designed the home to be the school of relationships. The dearest, the closest, the most intimate human relationship is between husband and wife. They then teach their children to value and nurture relationships. Properly taught and modeled , these skills will serve them for a lifetime.

↥↧ **Praying for My Circles Today**
Thank God for happy memories and meaningful relationships. Turn to page 90 and pray for your immediate-family members, especially those who are lost.

# *Day 3* • Broken Relationships

### God's Word for Today

"We love because He first loved us. If anyone says, 'I love God,' yet hates his brother, he is a liar. For the person who does not love his brother whom he has seen cannot love God whom he has not seen. And we have this command from Him: the one who loves God must also love his brother" (1 John 4:19-20).

 **Read and meditate on "God's Word for Today" in the margin and spend a moment in prayer as you begin today's lesson.**

Reflection on the importance of relationships will lead to obvious but amazing conclusions. Think about the crisis times of your life:

- As a child separated from your parents
- As a child angry with your parents
- As a teenager breaking up with your sweetheart
- The resentment and misunderstanding that separated you from a friend
- The emptiness and heartbreak of losing a parent or spouse
- An argument or maybe even divorce from your husband or wife
- A crisis with an employee or employer
- Times of resentment and rupture in the family
- Distress in business or in your church

 Identify two of your most dark, sad experiences and write the initials of persons who were involved in those experiences with you.

_____

_____

If you think about all of the dark, sad times in your life, you will realize that the vast majority of these times were created by ruptured, strained, or broken relationships.

Every broken business, every broken home, every broken friendship involves broken relationships. Every local, national, or international problem, every crime committed, and every war from the beginning of time has resulted from ruptured relationships.

When society ceases to treasure relationships, it becomes decadent. Manners become coarse and cheap. Common courtesy is soon forgotten. Hearts become thankless, ceasing to show appreciation. As human history so painfully demonstrates, bad relationships produce—

- broken marriages;
- broken homes;
- unsuccessful businesses;
- divided churches;

- weak governments;
- chaotic nations.

When believers experience broken relationships, they hinder the movement of the Spirit of God. They neutralize our witness and lessen its importance. Broken relationships shut off the divine well that can flow to all our world. To keep the divine well flowing, we Christians need to right all broken relationships.

Because of broken relationships, your conscience may not be clear. You may feel guilty over an offense, or you may feel like a hypocrite asking a person to be reconciled to God when you cannot reconcile with another person. Do whatever is necessary to right any broken relationships you may have. Then the Holy Spirit can have a clear channel through which to flow. To be prepared to share the gospel with others, you must get right with others.

(2) **Turn to "Your Horizontal Relationships with Others" on pages 104–5 and complete the inventory.**

(3) **If you could improve or be reconciled in one relationship in your life today, which one would it be?**

_____

**↕ Praying for My Circles Today**

Pray about the relationship you identified at the end of today's lesson. What do you sense God wants you to do to get that relationship right? Ask Him. Record His directions here:

_____

_____

_____

_____

_____

_____

# Day 4 • Restored Relationships

· · · · · · · · · · · · · · · · · · · · ·

## God's Word for Today

"Christ's love compels us, since we have reached this conclusion: if One died for all, then all died. And He died for all so that those who live should no longer live for themselves, but for the One who died for them and was raised. In Christ, God was reconciling the world to Himself, not counting their trespasses against them, and He has committed the message of reconciliation to us. Therefore, we are ambassadors for Christ; certain that God is appealing through us, we plead on Christ's behalf, 'Be reconciled to God'" (2 Corinthians 5:14-15,19-20).

**Read and meditate on "God's Word for Today" in the margin and spend a moment in prayer as you begin today's lesson.**

If all relationship problems were solved, there would be no divorce, no war, no employer-employee or labor-management disputes. Solve the relationship problems of the world, and humanity's most perplexing problems are solved, because right relationships produce solid marriages, stable homes, successful businesses, ministering churches, good governments, and strong nations.

We know that God wants to meet our needs. He builds beautiful relationships in the body of Christ. He intends that we love one another the way He loved us (see John 15:12). He wants to meet our needs through the body of Christ so that we will all be healthy parts of a functioning body. We need one another.

Jesus came to earth to meet our deepest need. He died on the cross to redeem the world to Himself. He ascended to heaven, and He left the body of Christ on earth to go out and enlarge the body and strengthen the body.

Let's say the church is a divine hospital. The world is full of sickness. Many, many people come to the hospital for help, and the church realizes that all of us need help. We continually need help.

1) **Describe a time when a relationship in your church helped you heal.**

_____

_____

## John 15:12

"This is My command: love one another as I have loved you."

We come and come and come to the church for help, and we receive it. The only tragedy is that if we do not mature and join the hospital staff and start meeting other people's needs, we become a liability, and the flow is always directed inward. So we stagnate, and that hurts the body of Christ.

After we have come for help and have received it, God wants us to go out and build relationships with others. Then we become part of the helping staff. When we reach out to meet another person's needs, we find that our own needs are met.

As God begins to use a person, He begins to knock down walls of resistance and bad attitudes in that person's life. Perhaps some relationships in your own life are not right. God wants to use even those relationships for His glory.

Often the first thing that comes to mind when we think about a ruptured relationship is, *If I am a Christian and I admit that I have been wrong, what will the other person think of me?* That is the voice of pride. Who cares what the other person thinks of you? The important thing is what God thinks of you when you are acting in obedience to get a relationship right. Also consider what the person will think of Jesus if you do not make the relationship right.

② **Is there a ruptured relationship in your life?** ○ Yes ○ No

③ **Read Matthew 5:23-24 in the margin. What did Jesus tell you to do about a ruptured relationship?**

_____

Matthew 5:23-24 says that even if your brother is upset with you, go to him and be the reconciler. Because you are the one who is living in victory, you are to be the reconciler.

By seeking to right wrong relationships, you keep your conscience clear. If the Holy Spirit brings something to your mind that is wrong in your life, set it straight. Deal with it. Keep short accounts with God and with others. In your personal walk with God, let Him work out His redemptive purpose in and through your life.

Sometimes I meet people who have difficulty with concentric circles because they do not want to reconcile relationships in those circles. But it is impossible to be right with God and wrong with those around us. Would you be willing to sacrifice a right relationship with God over any human relationship you have? If you would, then you really do not know God the way He wants you to know Him. Nothing could be more valuable than being right with God.

Your world needs you. People throughout your concentric circles need you. Be a channel of God's love. There is no greater thrill in life than letting the Lord love through you and meet needs through you. That is the Christian life.

I know hundreds of students who once had ruptured relationships with their parents but eventually led those parents to the Lord. Now they have liberty because the ruptures are healed. If you get right with others in your concentric circles, God's love can flow through you to forever change their lives for His glory.

**Matthew 5:23-24**
"If you are offering your gift on the altar, and there you remember that your brother has something against you, leave your gift there in front of the altar. First go and be reconciled with your brother, and then come and offer your gift."

**Praying for My Circles Today**
Look over your list of immediate-family members on page 90. Take time to pray for each person. Look for opportunities to share God's love with them.

## Day 5 • A Channel of Love

### God's Word for Today

"Dear friends, let us love one another, because love is from God, and everyone who loves has been born of God and knows God. The one who does not love does not know God, because God is love. God's love was revealed among us in this way: God sent His One and Only Son into the world so that we might live through Him. Love consists in this: not that we loved God, but that He loved us and sent His Son to be the propitiation for our sins. Dear friends, if God loved us in this way, we also must love one another. No one has ever seen God. If we love one another, God remains in us and His love is perfected in us" (1 John 4:7-12).

 Read and meditate on "God's Word for Today" in the margin and spend a moment in prayer as you begin today's lesson.

Jim came into my office one day and said, "Dr. Thompson, my dad is a nominal Christian; but when he learned that I was going into the ministry, he became furious. He told me that he did not mind my being a Christian, but he did not want me to become a 'religious nut.'"

Jim's father drove a truck for a large truck line, owned his own rig, and wanted his son to follow in his footsteps. Instead, Jim had come to the seminary. As a result, Jim's relationship with his parents was ruptured.

"We had been very close until this happened," Jim explained. "Since then I have just ignored them, as they have ignored me. It has hurt me, but I am going to serve Jesus. My family can do whatever they please."

I asked, "Jim, do you really think you can be right with God and have ruptured relationships with your parents? You need to meet their needs. You need to love them."

Jim answered, "Well, that's right; but I don't know what to do."

So I suggested that he start to pray for them and make the ruptured relationships right.

Jim began to pray for his dad and mom. That same day he came to class brokenhearted and said, "Friends, just please pray for me." Then Jim prayed, "Father, I do not even know if my daddy knows you. But Father, I have been wrong in my attitude toward my parents. Forgive me of my attitude and help me meet my parents' needs."

Jim wrote a letter to his parents, asking them to forgive him because of his bitterness and the broken relationship. He told them that he loved them.

The next day, before the letter had time to reach his parents, Jim received a telephone call from his dad. Jim's dad had never before had a route to Dallas, but he said, "Son, I have a route to Dallas this week, and I want to see you."

"Oh, Dad, that's great!"

That Saturday afternoon a big rig pulled up in front of Jim's dorm. When Jim opened the dorm door, his tall father stood with tears trickling down his cheeks. "Jim, I am wrong with God," he said. "Can you help me?"

When Jim got right with God, he also wanted to get right with his parents. Once God had prepared Jim, he brought Jim's dad to Dallas so that Jim's life could be a channel of love to point his dad to Jesus Christ.

1. **Do you have a family relationship that needs to be reconciled like Jim and his dad?** ○ Yes ○ No

    **If so, now may be the time to get right with others. Have you allowed pride to affect any of your personal relationships? If so, humble yourself and take the initiative to be reconciled to those you have offended by your pride.**

    **What do you need to do to be reconciled with the person?**
    ○ Write a letter
    ○ Make a phone call
    ○ Visit the person
    ○ Make restitution
    ○ Other: _____

    _____

    _____

    _____

    _____

    **After praying, go and obey the Lord. Let God set you free from bitterness, unforgiveness, or guilt over a broken relationship.**

 **Praying for My Circles Today**
Pray about any broken relationships in your life. Repent of any bitterness and unforgiveness on your part. Ask the Lord to enable you to take the actions necessary to be reconciled with others.

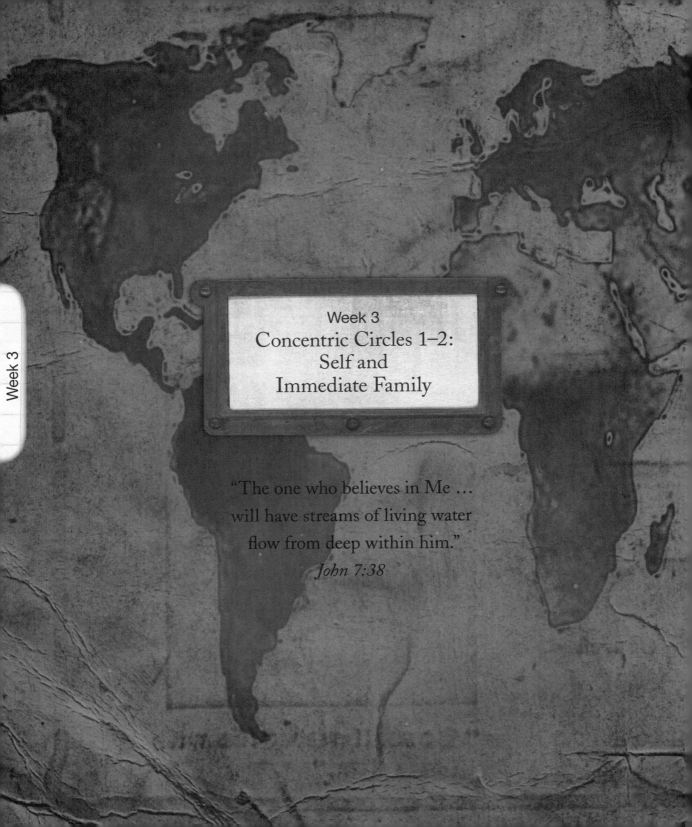

Week 3
Concentric Circles 1–2:
Self and
Immediate Family

"The one who believes in Me …
will have streams of living water
flow from deep within him."
*John 7:38*

There are two basic types of relationships in life. One is the vertical relationship we have with God, which is our most important relationship. The only way we can come to the Father is on His conditions.

The other basic type of relationship is the horizontal relationships we have with other people. God has laid down the basis for all of our other relationships. Accepting His conditions for relationships means that we forfeit forever the right to choose whom we love. The kind of love we will express has nothing to do with looks, age, shape, size, color, sweetness, hostility, or personality. Our job is to love anyone Jesus chooses to bring into our lives. When you establish by faith the proper vertical relationship with God as your Heavenly Father, you can then have right horizontal relationships with others and deal with the basic problems of the world.

This week we will start by focusing on that first and most important relationship—your relationship with God. When your vertical relationship with God is right, He will begin helping you get a proper perspective of who you are in Christ. He will help you get to know the real you. From this foundation of a right relationship with God and a strong and proper view of self, God can begin to flow through your life to others.

## OVERVIEW OF WEEK 3
Day 1: God's Design for You
Day 2: Circle 1: Get Right with Self
Day 3: The Need for Balance
Day 4: Circle 2: Immediate Family
Day 5: Meeting Needs at Home

## VERSE TO MEMORIZE
"The one who believes in Me, as the Scripture has said, will have streams of living water flow from deep within him" (John 7:38).

## DISCIPLESHIP HELPS FOR WEEK 3
Your Vertical Relationship with God (pp. 106–7)

# *Day 1* • God's Design for You

**God's Word for Today**

"The one who believes in Me … will have streams of living water flow from deep within him" (John 7:38).

 Read and meditate on "God's Word for Today" (this week's verse to memorize) in the margin and spend a moment in prayer as you begin today's lesson. Remove the Scripture-memory card from the back of your book and begin committing this verse to memory.

The first and foremost barrier that would hinder you from reaching out in love to people in your concentric circles is that perhaps you have never met the One who is love. Have you met Jesus? The beginning point for preparing to share the good news with others is a right relationship with Jesus Christ. You must first get right with God.

We are designed for fellowship with the King—God Himself. As birds were made for the air and fish for the sea, people were created for fellowship with God. Nothing will satisfy the deepest needs of our beings until we have fellowship with Him. This right relationship with God, in turn, will result in the right kind of fellowship with others on God's conditions.

You receive God's grace when you come to Him under His conditions. As a believer, you have to continue accepting those conditions every day. Colossians 2:6 says, "As you have received Christ Jesus the Lord, walk in Him." What does that mean? It means that as you have accepted Jesus Christ by faith, you walk with Him each day by faith.

With our five senses we perceive the world. We lock into our minds as knowledge what our five senses tell us. We can know about God mentally, so many people only know about God. They can state many concepts about God, but they do not know God by experience.

**Ephesians 2:1**

"You were dead in your trespasses and sins."

My body makes me world-conscious, my mind makes me self-conscious, and my spirit makes me God-conscious. But if my spirit is dead in trespasses and sin (see Ephesians 2:1), a holy God cannot be there. I still have a spirit, but it is dead toward God. In the new birth God breaks through and comes to dwell in me and makes me spiritually alive. I am then born from above.

The authority of the Christian life is no longer physical. When a Christian is born from above, the Spirit of God dwells in that person's spirit, flows through his mind, and moves through his body. Then we Christians "present [our] bodies as a living sacrifice, holy and pleasing to God" (Romans 12:1). Why? So that "the one who believes in Me … will have streams of living water flow from deep within him" (John 7:38).

When you are born again, you are alive to God. You are now the channel through which the Holy Spirit wants to move and manifest Himself to the world.

Perhaps you have deep needs in your life and are hurting. Remember that because God loves you, He has already made provision for every need in your life. His greatest provision is that He can forgive your sins. You can join the church, lead a moral life, help people, and give money to the church. But these actions cannot take away your sin.

Jesus Christ entered history and died to save us from our sins. He paid the price of death for our sins so that we can be forgiven. Jesus' death is God's provision for our need. Because of Him, we have eternal life. Everything has been done that is required for you to get right with God. You have to come to God on His conditions. If you have never done that, you will not be able to witness about the good news that Jesus saves.

**Pray and ask God about the true nature of your relationship with Him. How would you evaluate it?**
- ○ I don't have a relationship with Jesus Christ.
- ○ I don't have the kind of faith relationship with Jesus Christ that you described, but I would like to know Him that way.
- ○ I have a faith relationship with Jesus Christ, but I've strayed from closeness with Him. I need to repent of sin and return to Him.
- ○ I have a faith relationship with Jesus Christ and seek daily to walk in a right relationship with Him.

**If you don't have a relationship with Jesus Christ, follow the steps in the margin to establish that relationship.**

**If you have a relationship with Jesus, evaluate your fellowship with Him. Are you in agreement with Him in your daily walk? Are you obeying Him? Are you trusting Him daily to give you victory over sin? After doing this evaluation, if you recognize that the Holy Spirit is leading you to make changes, do it now. Repent of and turn away from any known sin. Choose afresh to make Christ Lord of your life daily.**

 **For guidance in identifying specific ways you might need to repent, turn to pages 106–7 and complete the inventory in "Your Vertical Relationship with God."**

## Establishing a Relationship with Jesus Christ

- Agree with God about your sin and your failure to measure up to His standards.
- Ask Him to forgive you, and to release you from the guilt of your past.
- Place your trust in what Jesus did for you by paying your penalty for sin on the cross.
- Invite Him to come into your life and become your Lord. Pledge to follow Him.
- If you need more help, talk to a Christian friend or a pastor.

## Praying for My Circles Today

Thank God for any commitments He has led you to make today. Ask for His help in walking in close fellowship with Him. Repent of any other sins He brings to your attention.

## Day 2 • Circle 1: Get Right with Self

**Read and meditate on "God's Word for Today" in the margin and spend a moment in prayer as you begin today's lesson.**

**God's Word for Today**

"You are a chosen race, a royal priesthood, a holy nation, a people for His possession, so that you may proclaim the praises of the One who called you out of darkness into His marvelous light" (1 Peter 2:9).

**Ecclesiastes 2:11**

"When I considered all that I had accomplished and what I had labored to achieve, I found everything to be futile and a pursuit of the wind. There was nothing to be gained under the sun."

Let's discuss self and what keeps the divine flow of God's love moving through it. No matter what methodology we use, if self is not right, we have problems. Self is your biggest problem and my biggest problem. In the natural economy of the self, we say, "I love me, and I want you to make me happy." Isn't that nice? As long as you meet my conditions, everything is going to be all right. The only problem with that is that it will not work!

All of us, you see, were born with the first Adam's nature. Its allegiance has three words, all personal pronouns: me, my, and mine.

1. **Read Ecclesiastes 2:1-11 in your Bible. In verse 11 how did the writer describe his achievements?**

_____

_____

This guy had "I" trouble. I, me, my, mine. He had a blank check, no limit, carte blanche. You say, "Wouldn't that be great?" Not necessarily.

You may ask, "What does all this have to do with evangelism?" Everything. There is a flow of life in every person. The flow is either through you or to you. Jesus told us that someone who believes in Him "will have streams of living water flow from deep within him" (John 7:38). But you see, life cannot flow through you when you always want it to flow to you. We cannot win the world around us when we are not sure about our own private world.

In relationships we learn to wear masks with people. We play games in our relationships by always changing our masks. With one person we are a certain way, with another person we are a different way, and in business we are a different way. We feel we have to act a certain way if we want to elicit a certain response from a client, an employer, or an employee. After a while we forget which mask we have worn with which person. Suddenly we switch masks and surprise or confuse them. How can others develop a meaningful relationship with an unreal person? You must allow God to help you become the real person He intends for you to be.

② **What masks have you worn in the past and for what purpose?**

_____

_____

God wants you to feel good about you. He doesn't want you to try and cover up the real you. The Scriptures say, "Love your neighbor as yourself" (Matthew 19:19). You cannot love others without first loving yourself. You have to feel good about you.

③ **What do you think it means to feel good about yourself?**

_____

_____

God wants you to feel good about you. He wants you to love you. That sounds strange, doesn't it? What do you do when you love you? The Bible tells husbands to love their wives as they love their own bodies (see Ephesians 5:28). Do you stand in front of the mirror and say, "Oh, I just love me"? No! When you love yourself, you meet your own needs. You feed yourself, cleanse yourself, brush yourself, shine yourself, paint yourself, clothe yourself, warm yourself, and cool yourself. Is there anything wrong with any of those things? Of course not. That is loving yourself. God wants us to take care of ourselves. Love is meeting needs.

④ **What evidence suggests that you love yourself?**
- ○ I take care of my physical needs.
- ○ I seek to grow spiritually.
- ○ I seek to grow mentally.
- ○ I take care of my physical health by exercising and eating right.
- ○ Other: _____

**What do you need to do to better meet your own needs?**

_____

_____

**Ephesians 5:28**
"Husbands should love their wives as their own bodies. He who loves his wife loves himself."

**Praying for My Circles Today**
Ask God to reveal any masks you are wearing before Him and others. Take off the masks in His presence and ask Him to mold you into the new creation He wants you to be.

## God's Word for Today

"If we confess our sins, He is faithful and righteous to forgive us our sins and to cleanse us from all unrighteousness" (1 John 1:9).

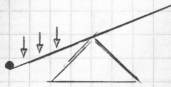

Pressures and problems push down on us.

The old nature uses wrong ways to get back up.

# Day 3 • The Need for Balance

 Read and meditate on "God's Word for Today" in the margin and spend a moment in prayer as you begin today's lesson.

The self seeks balance. Our lives are much like a seesaw. The problems of life come, and pressure pushes us down to make us think less of ourselves. We feel guilty, and this pushes us further down. That selfish sin nature wants to get back up.

All this begins to happen at an early age. All we want is to be balanced, but someone else gets on our little seesaw and begins to criticize us, to push us back down. Any kind of criticism causes immediate reaction. What do we do? If you hit me, I am going to hit you back! You criticize me, and I say that you are not so hot either. This is the natural, normal result of self-compensation: I am going to take care of me.

When someone tries to help us, we are sensitive and insecure. We think others are pushing us down, so we work to push ourselves back up again. When we begin to react toward other people, we begin to sense a feeling of control. If we have natural abilities, we use that control for our own selfish interests.

Here are some of the things people become when they react and respond to being pushed down.
○ The mask who hides the real person
○ The intimidator with an inferiority complex
○ The self-centered achiever
○ The topped-out achiever
○ The bottomed-out underachiever
○ The neurotic daydreamer
○ The psychotic who has escaped reality
○ The person who has created an alternate lifestyle looking for meaning
○ The alcoholic or drug addict who flees reality

1. Reread the previous list and check ways you have acted in the past because you were hurting and feeling bad about yourself.

If you are still living in one of these ways, decide to turn away from that false self and turn to the Lord. Ask Him to heal the brokenness or fill the emptiness. Ask Him to help you experience His love, forgiveness, and acceptance in such a way that your inferiority complex disappears. Ask Him to help you accept the person He created you to be. Ask Him to bring balance into your life.

How do we achieve balance? This is an oversimplification, but here it is: go to the cross. There we are clear and clean and balanced and do not have a running battle with anyone or ruptured relationships anywhere. If we are going to achieve the balance Jesus offers, we must come to the cross; die to self; die to me, my, and mine; and let Him be Lord. Jesus Christ brings balance to your life.

If someone blames us even though we are not guilty, we take that to the cross too. We do not let bitterness build up. You might say, "But he criticizes me all the time." So what? If you know who you are in Christ, who cares? If your Heavenly Father—the Creator of the universe—loves you, cares for you, and accepts you, that is enough! The person who is balanced is not devastated by criticism. He knows who he is in his relationship with God. He can rest in his relationship with Jesus Christ.

When you start living a holy life and God begins to love through you, some people will be upset. Because your lifestyle will rise higher than their lifestyles, they will feel bad about their lifestyles. Your lifestyle condemns theirs. Their inferiority complex gets irritated, and they try to put you down to start feeling better about themselves. They will start throwing rocks. You could get upset, but you just love them anyway.

Why do you want to achieve? God made you to be the best you can be, so don't feel guilty. Don't compare yourself to anyone else. You are like a snowflake. You are like a fingerprint. You are you. You are one of a kind. God made you to be you. And when Jesus fills you, you can accept you. You can be balanced.

God has a ministry for you, and He has a plan for you. Be faithful in the things you can do. You are not to judge yourself by your peer group. Do not be condemned by anybody else's standards. You are you.

Do not worry about your achievement level either. You achieve for the glory of God. As you achieve, you lay your successes at His feet. Do all you do for the glory of God.

If we can achieve that balance, we will achieve it at the cross. That is why I glory in the cross. That is why Jesus died for me. That is where I can find forgiveness of sin. That is where I do not have to blame anyone else. That is where God's goodness and love flow to me. That is where I find achievement. I do not have to be frustrated, comparing myself to other people. I am who I am.

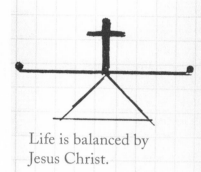

Life is balanced by Jesus Christ.

**Praying for My Circles Today**

Determine whether any of the following apply to you. Ask God to show you the truth of who He is for your situation.

- Someone blames, accuses, or corrects you for something for which you are guilty.
- Someone blames, accuses, or corrects you for something for which you are not guilty.
- You are so wounded or hurt that you want to run away or escape.
- Your inferiority complex attacks, and you feel worthless, unloved, inadequate, or inferior.
- You are driven to achieve.
- You despise who you are and envy someone else.

# *Day 4* • Circle 2: Immediate Family

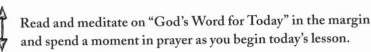

## God's Word for Today

"'Go back to your home, and tell all that God has done for you.' And off he went, proclaiming throughout the town all that Jesus had done for him" (Luke 8:39).

Read and meditate on "God's Word for Today" in the margin and spend a moment in prayer as you begin today's lesson.

As we move beyond self and circle 1, we make a survey of circle 2 and list the members in our immediate family. Here I list Carolyn, my wife, and Damaris, my daughter. Because my father has gone to be with the Lord and I am the only son, I also list my mother in circle 2. I am in constant contact with her. These three are my immediate family.

Your immediate family is those who live under your roof. If you are away from home and not married, your survey for circle 2 will include your mother and father. If you are married, your immediate family will be your spouse and children. The rest of your family will go in circle 3, relatives. We will discuss your survey of relatives in week 4.

Let me tell you how I try to meet my family's needs every day. First I ask myself, *What is my daily responsibility to my wife, Carolyn?* God has put me into her life, and I accept His conditions for my relationship with her. I am there to meet her needs, whatever those needs may be. A Christian marriage means I commit myself first to Jesus Christ and then to my wife. Because my commitment is first to Christ, I accept my wife on His conditions with all the immeasurable love He has. My attitude toward her is like Jesus' attitude toward the church. He loved it, and He poured out His life for it (see Ephesians 5:25).

I also have a daughter, Damaris. She is 14 years old. She is blond, green-eyed, and irrepressible. Damaris has learned a lot from hearing me speak, so when she really has a need, she sits down and very maturely explains what it is. Sometimes she comes popping through and says, "I have a need" and keeps going. It is like going through and dropping a 50-cent piece in the proverbial slot machine and pulling the lever. Who knows? Dad might be in the right mood, and she may hit the jackpot.

Then there is my dear 82-year-old mother. She loves everything in sight. What a precious soul she is. She has a ministry of writing. I suppose she writes close to one hundred letters a month. She does not write empty, sentimental notes. They are sweet, but they also meet needs. They uplift you and encourage the recipient.

One day I said, "How do you do it?"

She replied, "When I miss Oscar [my father], when I get lonely, when I get afraid, or when I become blue missing Oscar's touch or his voice, I find somebody who has a need. I allow the Lord to reach out to them through me. When I comfort others, God comforts me."

These three are my immediate family, my circle 2. "But," you may say, "your second circle does not have any lost people in it." That's right. But if you are not loving those in your second circle, you are surely not going to love those in circle 7 very well. You see, this lifestyle is loving the saved and the lost. My circle 2 is a place for me to practice loving others by meeting their needs. It's a place for me to help my family learn to show love by meeting needs in their concentric circles too.

If you are not the channel of God's love to meet the needs of those in your immediate family, who will be?

1) **In week 1 you listed your immediate-family members on page 90. Now complete a separate survey form for each person in your immediate family (the form may be duplicated as needed). Include as much information as you have available. Add to this survey as you discover more information that may be helpful to you.**

2) **Ask yourself,** *Have I knowingly omitted anyone from this circle because of a broken relationship?* **If so, go back and add that information.**

**Give that relationship to the Lord and ask Him what you need to do next.**

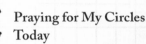

**Praying for My Circles Today**

Pray for each person in your immediate family. Ask the Lord to reveal their needs. Record these on your survey forms. Ask Him to teach you how to pray for and show love to each one. As you pray for each one, record on your survey forms any insights the Lord may give you.

# Day 5 • Meeting Needs at Home

### God's Word for Today

"Love is patient; love is kind. Love does not envy; is not boastful; is not conceited; does not act improperly; is not selfish; is not provoked; does not keep a record of wrongs; finds no joy in unrighteousness, but rejoices in the truth; bears all things, believes all things, hopes all things, endures all things Love never ends"
(1 Corinthians 13:4-8).

 **Read and meditate on "God's Word for Today" in the margin and spend a moment in prayer as you begin today's lesson.**

Love is meeting needs. If I am not allowing God to use me to meet my family's needs, my evangelism becomes hypocrisy. No wonder we don't want to share the gospel with the whole world. If it is not real at home, it is not going to be real out there either. God has given the home as the context in which we learn to build relationships.

Many students come to me in tears, saying, "I didn't do very well in high school. I didn't do very well in college. But I want to go into the ministry." I try to help them and encourage them; but tragically, those students lost a background in the school of knowledge. Education is a discipline, an opportunity to acquire tools you will use for the rest of your life. You can start building that foundation later in life. However, once you've wasted precious years, making up for lost time becomes more and more complicated the later you wait. The same principle applies to relationships. If we do not use the home as the basis for building relationships, we do not have the relational tools we will need later.

I shared this principle in class one day. Several days later, one of my students came to my office and said, "I really blew it. We have just started seminary, and my wife has been homesick. This is the first time she has ever lived a long distance from her family. Our house here is much smaller than the one we left. Yesterday she was just miserable. She said she didn't know what to do. I know God wants us here. I began to lecture her. I said, 'Honey, you know God has called us here. You know this is our calling.'"

The next morning in class God captured that student. The man said, "I did not meet my wife's needs." He went to her and asked, "Honey, will you forgive me? I am so blind that I do not even know what your needs are."

She said, "I was just lonely, afraid, and insecure in a new city, in a new life. I love you. All I wanted was for you to put your arms around me and hold me and say, 'Baby, it's all right!'"

Are there times when you need to take your child in your arms and just listen? Are there times when you need to turn the computer or television off and listen to your family? Learn their needs and then meet their needs.

Once I was teaching a night session for our seminary students' wives. We were talking about concentric circles. After our second meeting one of the wives asked to talk with me. She said, "My husband has been discouraged with one of his classes. I work all day long. I arrive at home after a hard day's work and rush to make dinner. Then I walk to our session. But after the evening session last week as I got to the door of our house, I had that ringing in my ears, 'Love is meeting needs! Love is meeting needs!'"

She continued, "The first thing I saw when I walked through the door was my husband sitting in his easy chair watching the football game."

He said, "Honey, will you bathe the kids and put them to bed?"

She said, "There were dirty dishes from dinner. The house was a wreck. He had done nothing all day long." She sighed and continued, "I took a deep breath. I did not feel very loving, but I decided to trust the Lord to love through me. What are his needs? Well, the first is for me not to create a scene." So she said to her husband, "I have wanted to see the children all day. This will give me an opportunity to be with them."

By the time she had changed clothes and went to get the children, she heard the bath water running. He had already begun bathing the children. He said, "If you will towel off this one, I will take care of the other one."

She continued, "You know, God began to do something in my heart toward my husband. There has been so much pressure between us lately, but now it all seems to be gone. I have come to realize that my own responsibility before God is to be His channel for meeting needs."

① **Have you been hurting silently because a family member seems to be overlooking your needs? Ask God how you can begin the flow of reciprocal love by loving him or her first. Ask the Lord for wisdom to know what to say, if anything, to let your family know of your need.**

What about children? Parents are to meet children's needs. We need to listen to our teens and hear from them what their needs are. We can't presume to know what those needs are; we must listen. Teens are crying out for love, for mothers and fathers to understand what they are going through.

We need to pray for our children. We need to pray for the Holy Spirit to speak to them, to convict them. But most importantly, we need to pray for the Holy Spirit to make us the kind of mothers and fathers our children need. We must pray that we will listen, that we will hear, and that we will meet their needs. There is no better success story in the world than that of a mother and father who can look at their baby who has developed into a man or woman and who radiates the character of Jesus Christ, who knows and cares about the needs of others. That is success!

## Praying for My Circles Today

What are some ways God wants you to love your immediate family? Take time now to pray for each family member. Ask the Lord what his or her needs are and what He would like to do through you even today to meet their needs. Check any of the following actions He is leading you to take.

○ Show grace and mercy by forgiving and restoring a broken relationship.

○ Show love by meeting a need or needs.

○ Ask the family member how you can pray for him or her.

○ Cultivate a closer relationship by building a relational bridge.

Take notes on your survey forms. As God reveals things He wants you to do, describe the project, need, opportunity, or action planned. Start meeting needs for God's pleasure.

Week 4

# Concentric Circles 3–6: Relatives, Friends, Neighbors, Associates, and Acquaintances

"This is My command:
love one another
as I have loved you."

*John 15:12*

Week 4

Just before His ascension into heaven, Jesus said to His disciples, "You will receive power when the Holy Spirit has come upon you, and you will be My witnesses in Jerusalem, in all Judea and Samaria, and to the ends of the earth" (Acts 1:8).

You have a Jerusalem—those closest to you. You have a Judea—a broader concentric circle. You have a Samaria—a still broader concentric circle.

Many people who have been Christians for a long time may not think they have relationships with people who are lost. We don't stop to think about all the people God brings into our lives or into our circles of influence. When believers begin to identify those in their concentric circles, they find all kinds of people who need the Lord.

Last week you began identifying and praying for persons in circle 2, your immediate family. This week you will identify people in the next four circles of influence and begin recording basic information about each person. First you'll look at your circle of relatives. Then you'll start identifying your friends, neighbors, business or school associates, and acquaintances. This survey will become a prayer list that will help you begin praying for those God has brought into your concentric circles of concern.

## OVERVIEW OF WEEK 4
Day 1: Surveys Are Your Strategy
Day 2: Circle 3: Relatives
Day 3: Circle 4: Friends
Day 4: Circle 5: Neighbors and Associates
Day 5: Circle 6: Acquaintances

## VERSE TO MEMORIZE
"This is My command: love one another as I have loved you" (John 15:12).

## DISCIPLESHIP HELPS FOR WEEK 4
Survey Forms: Circles 3–6 (pp. 92–99)
God's Activity Watch List (p. 108)

# *Day 1* • Surveys Are Your Strategy

### God's Word for Today

"This is My command: love one another as I have loved you" (John 15:12).

Read and meditate on "God's Word for Today" (this week's verse to memorize) in the margin and spend a moment in prayer as you begin today's lesson. Remove the Scripture-memory card from the back of your book and begin committing this verse to memory.

This week you will be asked to complete surveys for people in your circles of influence, as you did last week for your immediate family. You may ask, "Why is a survey necessary?" For the simple reason that you cannot remember everything you need to remember without writing it on paper. You need a structure for your evangelistic efforts. Nothing becomes dynamic until it becomes specific. As you take surveys on those in your circles of influence, you become conscious of people you never would have thought of. They are in your circle of influence for a reason, and perhaps they are in no one else's circle.

A pastor friend of mine presented concentric circles to his church. Church members began to complete their surveys and pray. In one month the church had 60 professions of faith. Doing a survey is important. It is the structure on which you build witnessing relationships.

1. **State in your own words why completing surveys for your concentric circles is important.**

_____

_____

_____

As you complete your surveys, remember that a witnessing lifestyle involves loving not only the lost but also the saved. Your concentric circles will include many people who are already saved. Do you pray for them? I hope so! They have needs and hurts too. Showing God's love to them is a way for you to practice loving others the way God wants you to love the lost world. Meeting their needs becomes a part of your lifestyle.

That's how I met my wife, Carolyn. At 27 I was the pastor of First Baptist Church in Sequin, Texas. I had gone all the way through Baylor University but had not found a wife. A dear friend called one day and asked me to come by his office to talk about visiting a family. Passing through his outer office the next day, I met his private secretary. Guess who? Carolyn. There she sat as I stumbled over the chair and the wastebasket and knocked the phone off the desk just getting from one door to the next.

When I finally made it to my friend's office, he handed me a sheet of paper with the family's name on it. "But wait," I said, "we will discuss that family later. Who is that beautiful creature?" I spent the next three weeks conducting an investigation like the FBI. I wanted to know everything I could about that girl. Then I planned my strategy. Now she is my wife!

When you care and God wants to care through you, you want to know about people. So complete your surveys. They become your strategy for reaching out with the love of Christ.

Once after I had introduced circle 3, relatives, to my class, a student named Jeff told me about his brother who had left home in the late 1960s with the hippy movement. His family had not seen him since. Jeff said, "He has broken my parents' hearts. We don't know whether he is dead or alive. I'm not sure I want to know what has happened to him. Can I leave him out of my circle 3?"

"No, Jeff," I answered, "God put your brother in your circle for a reason. Write his name down on your survey. Intercede for him."

As Jeff met God's conditions for a relationship with his brother, he received a deep burden to pray for him. Months passed, and nothing happened. But Jeff was faithful and continued to pray. Then all of a sudden an unexplainable circumstance drew this brother to Fort Worth. He called Jeff. Jeff called me at 2:30 a.m. after he had talked with his brother.

"Dr. Thompson, are you awake?"

"Well, I am now," I laughed.

Jeff then explained, "Dr. Thompson, this is Jeff. My brother just called. I've been praying, and here he is. He is coming to class with me in the morning."

"Good," I said. "Tomorrow I'll teach the class how to know Jesus in a personal way." And I did! And he did! Jeff's brother accepted the Lord in my office after class.

**Praying for My Circles Today**

Review the surveys you completed last week on your immediate family members (pp. 90–91). Add any information you may have omitted that would help you build relationships and pray for them. Spend time in prayer for your immediate family's specific needs.

## *Day 2* • Circle 3: Relatives

### God's Word for Today

"The Lord does not delay His promise, as some understand delay, but is patient with you, not wanting any to perish, but all to come to repentance" (2 Peter 3:9).

Read and meditate on "God's Word for Today" in the margin and spend a moment in prayer as you begin today's lesson.

Concentric circle 3 is assigned to relatives. That category can go on almost indefinitely, for it includes family members related to you by blood or marriage but do not live in the same house with you.

 In week 1 you listed your relatives on page 92. Turn to that page and make sure you included all of the following.

- Grandparents
- Parents
- Brothers
- Sisters
- Stepparents
- In-laws
- Aunts
- Uncles
- Grandchildren
- Nieces
- Nephews
- Cousins

Now fill out a survey form for each one, including as much information about them as you can. Start with those who are closest to your family.

When you complete surveys about your relatives and start praying for them, God will guide you to identify their needs. Then all you have to do is show an interest in and love for people. They will respond when they see that you care. That is living! Love is meeting needs!

Maybe you have so many relatives that you feel overwhelmed thinking that you need to pray for all of them. I realize that you cannot pray for each relative every day, but write their names on survey forms anyway. During your quiet time flip through your survey forms and pray as God leads you as you look at names. As you survey and pray for your relatives, you will begin to know who has needs at that particular time. God may cause you to become aware of needs as He invites you to join His work in their lives. It's very important to be close to your family so that you will be available for God's use.

One of my friends was completing surveys for circle 3 and remembered his great aunt Alice. Dick had met Aunt Alice several times at family reunions, but he was not sure where she lived. He wrote his mother and asked for her address.

Dick's mother reported that Aunt Alice, 82 years old, lived in a rest home about 85 miles from where Dick lived. She sent him the address, and on Aunt Alice's birthday Dick sent her a birthday card. Aunt Alice wrote back, thrilled to hear from him. In several weeks Dick called her to set up a time when he and his wife could visit her.

Dick introduced his wife to his aunt Alice, and they talked about the pleasantries of the day. Then Aunt Alice said, "Honey, tell me what you do."

"I am in Southwestern Seminary studying for the ministry," Dick answered.

Then Aunt Alice asked, "What do you study?"

Dick replied, "Basically, I study that the most important word in the English language, apart from proper nouns, is *relationship*—like the relationship we now have. I also study that if you really love someone, you meet that person's needs."

"Oh, that really sounds interesting; tell me more," Aunt Alice said.

Dick replied, "The basic need in the life of every individual is to know Jesus Christ in a very personal and intimate way."

"That sounds very interesting," she said. "Please tell me what you mean."

Dick then shared the gospel with her: how a person comes to know the Lord, how to have sins forgiven, and how to live in a right relationship with the Father and with others. Aunt Alice looked at Dick, big tears filling her eyes, and whispered, "Son, I've been a member of a church for years, but I've never done that. Could I trust Jesus?" As Dick and his wife knelt down beside that dear woman, she invited Jesus into her heart.

Months later when I saw Dick, he came up, put his arms around me, and said, "Doc, this weekend Aunt Alice went to be with the Lord." Then he added, "Dr. Thompson, what if I had not listed her in my concentric circles? What if I had not done my survey?"

I do not want to lay a heavy burden on you, but God wants you to take one day at a time. So redeem the time. Use it. You cannot win all of your family in one day. You have the rest of your life, however long that may be, to work through your concentric circles. But be available to God. Allow God to love through you to meet people's needs. The best way to start that process is to be intentional about it. Complete your surveys, pray for your relatives, and open yourself to ways God wants you to meet their needs.

## Praying for My Circles Today

Look at the survey forms you have prepared for your relatives. Begin praying for each person. Ask the Lord to begin revealing their needs. Ask Him to teach you how to pray for and show love to them. As you pray for each one, record on your survey form any insights the Lord may give you.

Ask yourself: *Have I knowingly omitted anyone from this circle because of a broken relationship?* If so, go back and add that person. Give that relationship to the Lord and ask Him what you need to do next.

## Day 3 • Circle 4: Friends

↕ **Read and meditate on "God's Word for Today" in the margin and spend a moment in prayer as you begin today's lesson.**

### God's Word for Today

"I am not ashamed of the gospel, because it is God's power for salvation to everyone who believes, first to the Jew, and also to the Greek" (Romans 1:16).

In concentric circle 4 are close friends. Sometimes friends are closer than relatives. In this circle you will include the people you spend time with, the ones you talk to about important things, the ones you participate with in hobbies or recreation activities. These are the people you could call in the middle of the night if you needed help, and they would gladly come.

① **Turn to page 94 and list your close friends—those you spend time with and really care about, trust, and can depend on. (Friends who are not as close can be included in circle 5, neighbors and associates.) Then prepare a survey form on each friend you listed. Begin making notes about ways you can reach out to them and meet their needs.**

Don't just wait to receive what you need from your friends. They have needs too. Watch for ways God may invite you to show His love for them by meeting their needs. If they are believers, you can practice Jesus' admonition to "love one another" (John 15:12). If they are unbelievers, pray that God's love through you will draw them to Christ.

### John 15:12

"This is My command: love one another as I have loved you."

Chris and Bill were best friends from the third grade through high-school graduation. Chris invited Bill to church activities and openly talked about his beliefs. Bill listened to his friend share that the most important word in the world is *relationships* and of the necessity of a vertical relationship with God. Bill patiently listened and said that at 16 he could not make that kind of commitment to follow Jesus. He understood that it would require a change in lifestyle, and he was unwilling to do so.

After their first year of college, Bill called Chris out of the blue, saying that he needed to talk. The first year of college had been crazy for Bill—fraternity parties, binge drinking, living on the wild side. Hitchhiking across the country, he encountered numerous Christians who talked to him again and again about making Jesus the Lord of his life. When he returned home, he immediately called his good friend Chris. Because of the groundwork Chris had laid in their relationship, Bill knew whom to ask when he wanted to know how to become a Christian.

2. **Who is your best friend?** _____
**Is that person a believer?**  ◯ Yes   ◯ No   ◯ I don't know

**If not, what needs to happen for God to use you to bring your friend to a saving relationship with Christ?**

_____

Our love for God must precede our love for the lost person. If we really love Him, we will love the ones He loves. We must realize the gravity of someone's lost condition without God. If we believe God's Word, we do not have another option. When Scripture says a person is lost without the Lord, it means exactly what it says. A person without Christ is lost and is headed for a Christless eternity in hell—even if that person is your closest friend.

3. **What would you most need to share with a lost friend? Check one.**
   ◯ a. If you will clean up your act, you can go to heaven.
   ◯ b. Jesus is the only way to heaven.
   ◯ c. There are many ways to get to heaven.

Some try to water down the gospel to make it easier to accept. But the thread of salvation through Jesus alone runs all the way through the Bible:
   • "No one comes to the Father except through Me" (John 14:6).
   • "There is salvation in no one else, for there is no other name under heaven given to people by which we must be saved" (Acts 4:12).
   • "The one who has the Son has life. The one who doesn't have the Son of God does not have life" (1 John 5:12).

If it did not take the death of Jesus Christ to redeem humanity, then the cross was a travesty. It was useless. No! He had to come and die. There was no other way. If He is the only way, then people are lost without Him. We need to weep over that. A person cannot be changed until he realizes, "Without Christ I am hopelessly and helplessly lost."

When you begin to think about close friends in circle 4, remember: if they are without Christ, they are lost and condemned to hell. We need to be concerned about their lostness. Because we do not know how long any of us have on earth, we must realize the urgency of confronting our friends with the gospel of Jesus Christ.

**Praying for My Circles Today**

Look at the survey forms for your close friends (pp. 94–95) and spend time praying for each one. Record ways God is directing you to reach out with His love. Pray that He will use you to meet their needs and especially to lead lost friends to Christ.

## Day 4 • Circle 5: Neighbors and Associates

### God's Word for Today

"You are called to freedom, brothers; only don't use this freedom as an opportunity for the flesh, but serve one another through love. For the entire law is fulfilled in one statement: You shall love your neighbor as yourself. But if you bite and devour one another, watch out, or you will be consumed by one another" (Galatians 5:13-15).

↕ **Read and meditate on "God's Word for Today" in the margin and spend a moment in prayer as you begin today's lesson.**

Concentric circle 5 includes neighbors, business associates, classmates at school, and not-so-close friends. In God's economy it is important to care about and build relationships with these people, just as you love and care for the people in circles 2–4. To do this, you will record information about them on surveys for circle 5. Why? Because you find out about people whom you care about.

For example, in the city it has become an increasingly greater problem to know our neighbors. But if love is meeting needs and if we want to meet their needs, we must know our neighbors. My neighbors will not believe that I want to be in heaven with them if I do not want them in my home for dinner or if I do not say hello when we are in our front yards. We have to know our neighbors before we can meet their needs.

1. **Turn to page 96 and list your neighbors and work or school associates. These are people you know and have an ongoing opportunity to interact with on a regular basis. Consider the following.**

   - Neighbors
   - Coworkers
   - Supervisors
   - Union members
   - Vendors
   - Clients
   - Subordinates
   - Classmates
   - Teachers
   - Fellow church members
   - Students
   - Teammates
   - Fellow club members

   **If you don't know their names, find out! Complete survey forms, recording as much information as you can about them.**

One of my friends told me a story that happened when he was a boy. One night he came home and saw his dad really working on something. Jim asked, "Dad, what are you doing?"

His dad replied, "I'm working on this telegraph key, learning the Morse code."

"Why?" asked Jim. "You aren't interested in ham radios."

"Yes, I am," his father replied. "You know Greg Smith's father down the street, the house with the big antenna?"

"Yes," Jim answered.

"I tried to reach him for Christ, but he wouldn't even talk to me," Jim's dad replied. "The only thing he knows and loves is ham radios. I'm going to learn how to be a ham-radio operator so that I can reach Greg's dad."

Jim's dad took the time to build a bridge to Greg's dad. That bridge was a ham radio. Six months later Greg's dad trusted Jesus. That is reaching out to your concentric circles and building bridges that will allow further communication and deepen your relationship.

2. **Choose one person in circle 5 and describe a natural way you could build a bridge to that person.**

_____

_____

After you have completed your surveys, have begun to intercede, and have made yourself available to God, you can build bridges to people by reaching out in love and showing them that you care.

A friend of mine lives across the street from a Korean couple. They are very quiet, and developing a relationship with them has been difficult. My friend said that after months of trying to build a relationship, the wife's mother died. My friend and his wife took the Korean couple a meal. They also took care of their pets and mowed their yard while they were out of town. When the couple came home, they said to my friend, "You have been so kind. We would like to be your friends."

Now these friends are ready to listen to the gospel from someone who has shown love to them. Love is meeting needs wherever we are.

Several years ago when I was near death, I learned something from the Lord that I will never forget: it is not how long I live; it is how I live. Methuselah lived 969 years and may have died in the flood of Noah's day. Enoch, his father, lived only 365 years. Then "Enoch walked with God, and he was not there, because God took him" (Genesis 5:24). Which would you rather be?

3. **Read "God's Activity Watch List" on page 108. Use these guidelines when relating to or praying about your concentric circles to identify in whose lives God is working.**

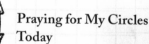

**Praying for My Circles Today**

Pray through the needs you have identified in circle 5. Ask God how He wants to use you to build bridges of communication and relationship. Consecrate yourself to be used in the ways He shows you. Record them on your survey forms. Then be obedient.

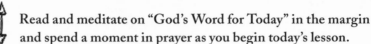

# *Day 5* • Circle 6: Acquaintances

## God's Word for Today

"Set apart the Messiah as Lord in your hearts, and always be ready to give a defense to anyone who asks you for a reason for the hope that is in you. However, do this with gentleness and respect, keeping your conscience clear, so that when you are accused, those who denounce your Christian life will be put to shame" (1 Peter 3:15-16).

Read and meditate on "God's Word for Today" in the margin and spend a moment in prayer as you begin today's lesson.

Concentric circle 6 is reserved for your acquaintances—people you know casually. For example, when you go to a grocery store or a restaurant, the checkers and waitresses may wear name tags. Those are not there just for decoration. They bear the names of people who are your acquaintances. We know their faces, and we need to be sensitive to their names as well. One of the deepest needs of any individual is for recognition. One way to give recognition to a person is to call her by name. When you call someone by name, you show that you value her and that you are concerned enough to remember her name. Remembering a name may not seem like much, but it means you care. You meet a need every time you say a person's name.

As your concentric circles become a lifestyle, you will begin to realize how important names are. When you call acquaintances by name, they will never forget you. You immediately build a bridge to a relationship.

1. List your acquaintances on page 98—people you bump into occasionally, usually for short periods of time. Consider people you meet at the grocery store, the gas station, restaurants, the gym, school, church, the dry cleaner, government agencies, neighborhood associations, and sports events. Complete a survey form on each person. You may not be able to list much information about them, but you can add to your survey as you build the relationship.

Meeting needs has a wonderful by-product. When you love other people, God gives dividends. You receive love from God and others.

One night a teenage girl charged into my office. She was a redheaded, vivacious, never-hit-the-ground type of personality. She plunked down in a chair and sobbed, "Pastor, I'm so unhappy. Nobody loves me."

I said, "Brenda, I know your parents. I know they are busy with their new business, but they love you. I know your friends. They love you."

"No, they don't," she replied. "Nobody loves me. I could die, and nobody would care."

I said, "God has created you as a channel for love to flow through you to others. The reason you may be miserable is that you want the flow to go the wrong way. When the flow of love is going the right way, as you were designed, you will not feel this way. You are supposed to do the loving. The person who always has to have the stream of love flowing inward is going to become a stagnant pool."

I suggested that Brenda find some people out there and meet their needs. "You don't have to feel good about loving them," I explained. "You don't have to have any feeling. From the heart you just make a decision: 'Dear God, whatever people You put in my path, I am going to show Your love by meeting their needs.'"

I continued, "Tomorrow I want you to make yourself available to Jesus. Get alone with Him. Then love somebody. Who out there would be really difficult for you to love?"

Immediately she replied, "Judy."

"Who is Judy?" I asked.

"Judy is a freshman," Brenda said. "She rides the bus with me, and she just bugs me. I have to ride with her 45 minutes every day. She crawls on the bus, and it's chatter, chatter, chatter. I just don't want to listen to that freshman. She latches on to me. I'm a senior."

I responded, "Assignment number one is for you to love Judy. That's my prescription."

Brenda came back Sunday and told me this story: "I got on the bus Thursday morning. No sooner than I sat down, Judy came and sat down beside me. It just really bugged me. I said, 'Lord, I'm going to meet her needs if it kills me.' The best thing I thought I could do was just listen. So I turned to her, and for the first time I looked at her while she was talking to me. As I looked at her, I began to see a little face I had never noticed before. I realized that underneath all that chatter was a hurting little girl.

"As we continued to talk, I asked, 'Judy, tell me about your brothers and sisters and mom and dad.' She became very still and quiet and was silent for a while. Finally, she said, 'Brenda, my mom and dad are getting a divorce, and I'm so scared. We have to move, and my whole world is coming apart.'"

Brenda said, "Pastor, in that moment I just listened. That's all I did, but I felt the love of God wanting to meet that little girl's needs through me. I put my arm around her, and we talked until we arrived at school. After getting off the bus, Judy put her books on the ground, put her arms around me, and said, 'Oh, Brenda, I just love you.'"

Do you have an acquaintance in circle 6 who bugs you? Perhaps the person has a deep problem. Perhaps you need to reach out and be sensitive to that person's need. Who is going to help him if you don't?

**Praying for My Circles Today**

Look over your acquaintances in circle 6 (pp. 98–99). Begin asking God to help you learn their names, build relationships, and learn their needs. Ask Him to give you love and compassion for each individual on your list. Is there a problem person on your list? Pray for that person and ask God how He wants you to love that person by meeting needs.

Week 5
Prayer and
Building Bridges

"I have become all things to all people,
so that I may by all means save some."
*1 Corinthians 9:22*

Prayer is not just a religious activity you do before you begin your work for the Lord. Prayer is a relationship with the Master of the universe. When you pray, you enter the throne room of heaven, where decisions are made that govern the universe. God invites us to pray so that when He answers, we will know He did it. He will receive glory.

This week we will explore the crucial role of prayer in cultivating relationships and seeking to win the lost. You will learn to pray for wisdom and discernment as you seek to meet needs and share Christ. You will learn to pray that God will engineer circumstances in the lives of others to draw them to Himself and to His Son, Jesus Christ. You will pray for the people in your surveys and watch to see where God is working in their lives. Then you can join God and show His love to the needy person.

You will also learn ways to build bridges through your relationships with lost people. Building relationship bridges is a key tool in a witnessing lifestyle. Continually building relationship bridges to your family, relatives, friends, neighbors, associates, acquaintances, and even to Person X keeps you attentive to their needs. Then you will have opportunities to reach out in love and to share Christ with those who need to know Him.

## OVERVIEW OF WEEK 5
Day 1: Intercession: The Greatest Work
Day 2: Be Specific
Day 3: Build Bridges
Day 4: Building Bridges in Times of Loss
Day 5: Show God's Love by Meeting Needs

## VERSE TO MEMORIZE
"I have become all things to all people, so that I may by all means save some" (1 Corinthians 9:22).

## DISCIPLESHIP HELPS FOR WEEK 5
Your Most Wanted (p. 109)

# *Day 1* • Intercession: The Greatest Work

## God's Word for Today

"I have become all things to all people, so that I may by all means save some" (1 Corinthians 9:22).

**1 Thessalonians 5:17**
"Pray constantly."

Read and meditate on "God's Word for Today" (this week's verse to memorize) in the margin and spend a moment in prayer as you begin today's lesson. Remove the Scripture-memory card from the back of your book and begin committing this verse to memory.

The one indispensable ingredient in a close walk with God is knowing how to pray. But real prayer is more than asking God to bless a meal, praying before a Sunday School class, or pulling the alarm of prayer in a time of trouble. We need to pray with intensity in emergencies, but someone who wants to witness to the world must "pray constantly" (1 Thessalonians 5:17), as Paul did. We need to continually pray through our concentric circles and trust that Sovereign God is working through circumstances to draw people to Himself. Keep in mind that He wants them to be saved more than you do. Prayer aligns your heart and will with God's desire to save them.

Believing in a supernatural God does not mean that you become passive and do not do anything. No, you are moving out to make a difference in your world; but as you go, remember that you are God's instrument. He sets your course. Your job is to intercede—that is, to pray for people—and to meet needs as God reveals them in your relationships.

1. Look over your survey forms for circles 2–6. List three ways God has answered your prayers for people in your concentric circles since you began this study.

1. _____

2. _____

3. _____

Can you imagine what would happen if your church used concentric circles as its outreach program? Members would complete surveys on their relationships and begin to intercede every day. Intercession would become a lifestyle for your church. Ruptured relationships would be made right. Members would show God's love to people in the community, and hearts would turn to Christ. We would go into worship services expecting God to work in hearts and lives.

Dick, one of my students, went out to pastor a little country church. The church had been there for many years, and members planned to remain there forever. But they did not plan to do anything.

Dick said, "Dr. Thompson, what should I do? I preach, but nothing happens. I want them to pray, but they don't want to. They say they hired me to pray. I want them to go visiting, but they don't want to go visiting because they say visiting is my job."

So I said, "Dick, why don't you share concentric circles with them?" He did.

Afterward one of the deacons said, "Preacher, I have a son who was married in this church last summer. He and his bride have not been back since. I had not even thought about it. I'm going to put them down in my circles and pray for them."

Then a grandmother said to Dick, "You know, I have a granddaughter who is 14. She has never made a profession of faith. I'm going to pray for her." Several others told Dick that the message had reminded them of someone to pray for.

As these individuals interceded for those in their concentric circles, this little church had 17 people who gave their lives to Christ, doubling the size of the congregation! The people were so excited that they kept adding to their surveys. They had caught the vision of how intercession could produce a hunger for the gospel among those in their concentric circles of concern.

 Now that you have done your surveys and have been interceding for several weeks, it's time to plan ways to pray more systematically for the people in your concentric circles. One suggestion is to pray for a different circle each day of the week. Or pray for a long and a short circle each day. Or divide your circles into 30 groups and pray for one group each month. It does not matter as long as you have a plan. Develop your prayer plan now. Then outline your plan below.

_____

_____

_____

_____

**Praying for My Circles Today**

Develop your prayer plan as suggested at the end of today's lesson. Begin praying according to your plan. As you pray, ask the Lord to reveal to you the needs of those in your circles. Ask Him to teach you how to intercede for them.

# Day 2 • Be Specific

## God's Word for Today

"First of all, then, I urge that petitions, prayers, intercessions, and thanksgivings be made for everyone, for kings and all those who are in authority, so that we may lead a tranquil and quiet life in all godliness and dignity. This is good, and it pleases God our Savior, who wants everyone to be saved and to come to the knowledge of the truth" (1 Timothy 2:1-4).

### James 4:2

"You do not have because you do not ask."

### Philippians 1:9

"I pray this: that your love will keep on growing in knowledge and every kind of discernment."

### James 1:5

"If any of you lacks wisdom, he should ask God, who gives to all generously and without criticizing, and it will be given to him."

**Read and meditate on "God's Word for Today" in the margin and spend a moment in prayer as you begin today's lesson.**

As you intercede for the people in your circles of concern, do not pray in blanket generalities. God expects us to pray for specific things. If you do not pray specifically, "you do not have because you do not ask" (James 4:2). How will you ever know if God answers prayer unless you pray specifically?

As you pray through your concentric circles, be sensitive to the Holy Spirit's leadership to draw your attention to those who have the deepest needs. Although several hundred people may be on your survey forms, God will help you know when and how He wants you involved with a particular person. When you become aware of a need, that awareness may be your invitation to join God's work in that person's life. If you sense a particular burden for someone while praying, you may want to call or write to that person and see what needs surface from that contact.

Paul showed us how to intercede. He said, "I pray this: that your love will keep on growing in knowledge and every kind of discernment" (Philippians 1:9). Paul specifically prayed for the Philippians to have wisdom and insight to meet people's needs through their love. Have you ever prayed Philippians 1:9 for anyone? Have you ever prayed for God's wisdom to meet another person's needs?

When you pray, pray for wisdom. You may ask, "Holy Father, give me wisdom to deal with this person." God will give it. When you pray for wisdom, do not sit around waiting to feel wise. Begin to move. As you go, God will supply the wisdom you need: "If any of you lacks wisdom, he should ask God, who gives to all generously and without criticizing, and it will be given to him" (James 1:5).

Remember, though, that before we can pray effectively for others, we have to be right with the Lord. We have to take self (circle 1) before the Lord and clear out the sin in that circle; then we can give attention to circles 2–7.

Do you want to intercede for others? Start with your relationship with God. Let me suggest a pattern for your prayers.

• "Lord, make me a clean channel for Your love."
• "Give me godly wisdom."

- "Father, engineer circumstances in their lives to draw them to You. Create circumstances through which I can love them and meet their needs."
- "Lord, make me available."
- "Lord, make me aware of their needs and show Your love through me as I seek to meet their needs.
- "Give me boldness to engage them with Your love and message of forgiveness."

 **Is there a relationship in your life that requires wisdom on your part? Use the suggestions above to pray for that person and for yourself. You may want to copy this list on a card to guide your prayers until this pattern becomes second nature to you.**

Follow up your prayers with loving actions. Some people may not immediately respond to you in love, so don't expect them to. Sometimes people do not know what to do with your love because they have never really been loved. Consequently, when you do something loving toward them and meet their needs, they may wonder what you want from them.

Regardless of the way the person responds to you, keep loving. Be genuine and do not expect too much too quickly. Make yourself available to God as He leads. After a while, others will learn that you really care. Meet their needs and ask God for wisdom as you work with them.

As you intercede and ask for wisdom, also ask God to engineer circumstances to draw people to Him. Sometimes it gets cloudy and dark when you start doing this. Sometimes a crisis comes, but do not let that alarm you. Sometimes darkness increases before the light breaks through. Sometimes it is a desert for months. But keep loving as you keep praying.

① **Turn to page 109 and list people whose salvation you need to pray for every day—your Most Wanted. This list should include lost persons in your immediate family as well as persons God has given you a special burden to reach.**

 **Praying for My Circles Today**

Use the prayer plan you developed in day 1 (p. 59) to pray for the appropriate concentric circles today. Also pray for your Most Wanted. Remember to pray for specific needs.

## *Day 3* • Build Bridges

### God's Word for Today

"Although I am free from all people, I have made myself a slave to all, in order to win more people. To the Jews I became like a Jew, to win Jews; to those under the law, like one under the law—though I myself am not under the law—to win those under the law. To those who are outside the law, like one outside the law—not being outside God's law, but under the law of Christ— to win those outside the law. To the weak I became weak, in order to win the weak. I have become all things to all people, so that I may by all means save some" (1 Corinthians 9:19-22).

Read and meditate on "God's Word for Today" in the margin and spend a moment in prayer as you begin today's lesson.

Building bridges is simply meeting needs in a person's life or showing an interest in them in such a way that you establish or cultivate a relationship. A relational bridge is a structure that allows you to cross from one side to another. For Christians, building a bridge is building a relationship that lets you cross into another person's world. Building a bridge makes the other person feel safe. Later the person will feel comfortable crossing into your world. The process of building bridges creates a relationship.

1. Read again 1 Corinthians 9:19-22 in the margin. Underline the reason the apostle Paul built relational bridges to people.

Paul built relationships to bring others to salvation in Christ. He did this by trying to identify with the needs and lifestyle of individuals around him.

Sometimes your relationship with someone is so shallow or distant that you have no way to reach out to the person in love. When you become aware of a person who needs the Lord, your job is to intentionally begin building a relational bridge so that God's love can flow to him or her.

2. Look at your concentric circles and list in the margin some persons with whom you are intentionally building witnessing relationships.

Building relationship bridges should be a continual process in your life. It should become a part of your lifestyle. The closer we are to the Lord, the more person-oriented we will become. Continually building relational bridges to our family, relatives, friends, neighbors, associates, acquaintances, and even to Person X is a significant strategy for witnessing to the world. Not only do bridges allow you to share Christ with others, but they also allow you to experience more of the abundant life Jesus came to give you. In addition, when people come to Christ through existing relationships with Christians, they are far more likely to follow through in establishing a growing relationship with a church—probably your church.

Doing something like sending a birthday card may be a great way to start your lifestyle of bridge building, but it is only a start. The process is a continual one. We should utilize as many points of contact as possible in bridge building. We need to become experienced master bridge builders. How do you begin to build bridges? When you sense that God wants you to reach out to someone, begin looking for points of contact with the person. If you do not have a point of contact, create one by asking questions, listening, and discovering things that interest him. If you can get on the same wavelength with him, you can begin establishing a relational bridge.

You can build relationship bridges to people in a variety of ways. You can show an interest in them during times of joy or stress. You can build bridges through shared interests or hobbies. One of the best ways to build a relationship is to rejoice when the person has an occasion to rejoice.

3. **As you read the following examples, think of people in your concentric circles whom you could reach through these ideas. Write their names in the margin beside the ideas.**

*The birth of a baby.* A wonderful way to touch someone's life is to show attention and consideration when a baby is born. Gifts and cards can express your interest at this time, but personal expressions of interest make greater impressions. Visiting in the hospital shows far more interest than sending a card. When mother and baby go home from the hospital, think of ways you can meet the family's needs. Take a meal. Clip a birth notice out of the local paper, laminate it, and send it with a note. Send flowers. Or volunteer to babysit one night so that the new parents can have a break.

*Birthdays.* Sending birthday cards is another important way to build bridges. A birthday is a very special day. Include your business associates, business partners, business contacts, colleagues, and employees.

*Congratulations.* Showing people that they are special builds bridges. Congratulate people for promotions, anniversaries, marriages, and graduations. Be creative. If teenagers win a district competition or a football game and are featured in the newspaper, cut the notice out of the paper, circle it in red, and write on it, "That's great. I'm proud of you." Sign your name and send them the clipping. You will have an open door into their world.

4. **List three persons on your Most Wanted list (p. 109) and write one idea for building a bridge to each person. Then follow through with your plan.**
   1. _____
   2. _____
   3. _____

**Praying for My Circles Today**

Remember to follow your plan for praying through your concentric circles. Pay special attention to your Most Wanted list (p. 109). Ask the Lord to reveal ways you can build relational bridges with the people for whom you are praying. Write notes on your survey forms as God gives you ideas or insights for reaching out to a person.

# Day 4 • Building Bridges in Times of Loss

 **Read and meditate on "God's Word for Today" in the margin and spend a moment in prayer as you begin today's lesson.**

### God's Word for Today

"Blessed be the God and Father of our Lord Jesus Christ, the Father of mercies and the God of all comfort. He comforts us in all our affliction, so that we may be able to comfort those who are in any kind of affliction, through the comfort we ourselves receive from God. For as the sufferings of Christ overflow to us, so our comfort overflows through Christ. If we are afflicted, it is for your comfort and salvation; if we are comforted, it is for your comfort, which is experienced in the endurance of the same sufferings that we suffer" (2 Corinthians 1:3-6).

Yesterday we talked about building bridges of relationship. Utilizing your points of contact can make a world of difference in others' lives.

One of my first pastorates was in a new mission church. Because the roads were gravel, they were dusty and noisy. Rocks flew when the members drove to and from church. I decided the roads should be paved.

The construction-crew supervisor who did the paving job was a big, likable man named Gus. When the job was done, I wrote him a long letter of appreciation and told him what a fine job he and his crew had done and how much I appreciated it. A few days later Gus's wife stopped me in town. She stood there a moment as big tears welled up in her eyes. She said, "Gus has worked for the city for years, and no one has ever written him a letter of appreciation. He read your letter over and over and just cried."

The next Sunday Gus and his wife were in church. Until this time neither had been in church. Six weeks later I baptized both of them.

Several months later Gus died of a heart attack. A letter of appreciation opened the door to a relationship with Jesus Christ. Expressing appreciation and care is a powerful way to build bridges.

1. **Identify a lost person in your concentric circles to whom you can express appreciation. Who will it be? What will you thank them for? Decide how and when you will express appreciation.**

---

Building bridges takes time, but nothing bears more fruit. In addition to the times of joy that we examined yesterday, times of stress and loss provide opportunities to build a relationship. Here are some examples.

*Sickness.* When people are ill and especially if they are in critical condition, they are open to your outreach and often to a relationship with God. Always visit lost people you know who are sick or in the hospital. Before making hospital visits, learn the do's and don'ts of visiting sick people. Your pastor or another staff member should be able to guide you.

*Sorrow.* You have a tremendous opportunity to build relational bridges when you reach out and love people during times of sorrow. Sometimes we do not know what to say when someone loses a loved one, but remember that what you say is not as important as the fact that you care. Sometimes you do not need to say anything. Being there says enough. When people are hurting, they will remember that you cared enough to come. Your presence itself will make a significant and perhaps lasting impression.

Remember to be attentive to surviving family members in the weeks following a loss. Sometimes the pressure and grief hit hardest several weeks after the funeral, when decisions have to be made. Often at this time the person needs a good listener. Send prayer notes, make occasional phone calls, drop by for a visit, or take the person out to lunch or dinner. Just providing an opportunity to talk about the loss can be very healing.

Put the date of the person's loss on your calendar for next year and contact them on the anniversary of the loss. That is another time when they will need comfort. You may also want to make a contact during the first year around holidays and anniversaries. At those times memories are strong, and grief may be difficult to handle. A friend who remembers these occasions means much to a grieving person.

*Stress.* Anytime you can reach out and build bridges to people in times of stress, they will never forget you. Such times may include a financial reversal, the loss of a job, or a crisis in the marriage or with children.

②  **Look over your concentric circles and try to identify at least one person who is experiencing one of the following.**
Sickness: _____
Sorrow: _____
Stress: _____

**Write what you will do to reach out to one or more of these persons.**

_____

As you pray for those in your concentric circles, watch for and seek times to build relational bridges. Keep your eyes and ears open to opportunities that may arise in your daily routine. Trust that God will call them to your attention also. Building relational bridges through your concentric circles is the key to witnessing to your world. A person's deepest need is Christ. As you build bridges, opportunities will open for you to share the good news of Jesus.

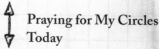 **Praying for My Circles Today**
Ask God to show you what you can do to build bridges to the people you identified in activity 2. Also pray for their specific needs.

# *Day 5* • Show God's Love by Meeting Needs

 **Read and meditate on "God's Word for Today" in the margin and spend a moment in prayer as you begin today's lesson.**

### God's Word for Today

"Little children, we must not love in word or speech, but in deed and truth" (1 John 3:18).

### Matthew 25:35-40

"'I was hungry and you gave Me something to eat; I was thirsty and you gave Me something to drink; I was a stranger and you took Me in; I was naked and you clothed Me; I was sick and you took care of Me; I was in prison and you visited Me.' Then the righteous will answer Him, 'Lord, when did we see You hungry and feed You, or thirsty and give You something to drink? When did we see You a stranger and take You in, or without clothes and clothe You? When did we see You sick, or in prison, and visit You?' And the King will answer them, 'I assure you: Whatever you did for one of the least of these brothers of Mine, you did for Me.'"

One of the best ways to be used by God in reaching your world is to show God's love. Love is meeting needs. As God engineers circumstances in the lives of those for whom you are praying, He will create an opportunity for the person to experience His love through your life. As He loves the person through you by meeting his or her needs, He will begin drawing that person to His Son. God engineers the circumstances so that His love can be shown. He works in your heart to motivate you to love a person who may not be very lovely. He also provides the resources to meet needs through you.

Your life becomes a channel of God's love. When you allow God's love to flow through you in this way, people will experience God. They will know that the Heavenly Father loves them. They will begin to sense His invitation to become a part of His family by adoption and by the saving grace of His Son.

Jesus said that the first and greatest commandment is to love God with all our hearts and souls and minds (Matthew 22:37-38; Mark 12:30). You might ask, "How do I love God?"

One morning after a class, one of my students, Rob, said to me, "I'm not really sure I understand something. I understand that love is meeting needs and that God wants to meet even the deepest need of people through me. But the first and great commandment is to love the Lord God with all our hearts, souls, and minds. The Bible says to love the Lord first, but how do I love God? He doesn't have any needs. How can I show God that I love Him?"

I said, "Matthew 25:35-40 gives us the answer to that question.

1 **Read Matthew 25:35-40. Underline ways we show we love God.**

When you love people in Jesus' name, you are loving Jesus. When those who are precious to Jesus become precious to you, you are loving God with all your heart and soul and mind. You are not really loving Jesus until you become a channel of His love in meeting needs. Love is meeting needs.

Matthew 22:39 and Mark 12:31 tell us that the second great commandment is "Love your neighbor as yourself." So you may ask, "How do we love people?" We are to love people the same way God loves people—by meeting their needs.

②  **Think about or look at your concentric circles. Note in the margin some ways you have met others' needs since you began this study.**

Loving others includes even your enemies. Jesus said, "You have heard that it was said, Love your neighbor and hate your enemy. But I tell you, love your enemies and pray for those who persecute you" (Matthew 5:43-44). How do you love your enemies? By treating them the same way you treat those you love. Love is treating all people the same way. When Jesus becomes the Lord of your life, you forfeit forever the right to choose whom you will love.

In your concentric circles you will find people who are not lovely. They may be cantankerous and unreceptive to a relationship with you. But you must pray, "Father, reveal their needs to me. Here I am. You know all the responsibilities I have, but wherever I go and whomever my life touches, I will be salt. I will be salt to touch and preserve, to help and heal and love. I will also be light to show the way to the Savior" (see Matthew 5:13-14). When you find someone who seems to be impossible to love, pray, "Father, engineer circumstances in his life to draw him to You, to meet his need."

**Matthew 5:13-14**
"You are the salt of the earth. … You are the light of the world."

  **Would someone in your concentric circles qualify as your enemy? Stop and pray for that person as suggested in the previous paragraph. Open yourself to God's use in reaching that person.**

Opening yourself to God's use this way will cost you, just as it cost Jesus to go to the cross. Remember, love is action. Love is meeting needs.

③  **What will you do to start meeting needs in your enemy's life?**

God's plan for your life is that His love flow through your life, reach out to others, and meet their needs. You do not meet their needs from your reservoir. You meet needs from God's reservoir. Your resources and your love are from God, and you must draw them from Him. That's why your love for God must precede your love for the lost. If you love God, you will love those He loves. To love without action, without meeting needs, is not love. Jesus always expressed His love for people by meeting their needs.

Maybe you object that your own needs aren't being met, so why should you meet somebody else's? Go to the cross and die to self. Romans 6–7 says you must die to self and let Jesus live through you. Then He funnels His love through you. You'll find that when you are meeting others' needs, your needs will also be met.

**Praying for My Circles Today**
Pray, "Father, fill me from Your great reservoir of love. I'm depending on Your love to flow through me to meet the needs of those around me." Then pray for those in your concentric circles according to the plan you have established. Allow God to meet needs through you.

Week 5 » Day 5

67

Week 6
# Person X
## and the
## Ends of the Earth

"All authority has been given to Me in heaven and on earth.
Go, therefore, and make disciples of all nations, baptizing them
in the name of the Father and of the Son and of the Holy Spirit,
teaching them to observe everything I have commanded you.
And remember, I am with you always, to the end of the age."

*Matthew 28:18-20*

Before He ascended to heaven, Jesus commissioned His followers to go and make disciples of everyone on earth (see Matthew 28:18-20). His Great Commission still applies to His followers today. As impossible as it sounds, believers are responsible for reaching the whole world with the life-saving gospel of Jesus Christ.

How can you reach the whole world? By meeting needs in your own world—in your own circles of influence. You can love your immediate family, your relatives, your friends, your neighbors, your associates, and your acquaintances. As you are obedient, the Lord will widen your concentric circles to encompass the Person Xs you meet each day and to see the great needs that exist at the ends of the earth. Your job is to keep loving all the people God brings into your life as your circles grow ever wider. Someday the Lord will ask you, "What did you do to reach your circles of influence?"

Does it still sound impossible? It's true that you cannot give from your own resources and meet all the needs God brings into your life; they are not sufficient. However, you can give from Jesus' resources. God plus you always equals enough.

## OVERVIEW OF WEEK 6
Day 1: Circle 7: Person X
Day 2: Reaching Out Through Circumstances
Day 3: Missions Awareness
Day 4: Missions Support
Day 5: Missions Involvement

## VERSE TO MEMORIZE
"All authority has been given to Me in heaven and on earth. Go, therefore, and make disciples of all nations, baptizing them in the name of the Father and of the Son and of the Holy Spirit, teaching them to observe everything I have commanded you. And remember, I am with you always, to the end of the age" (Matthew 28:18-20).

## DISCIPLESHIP HELPS FOR WEEK 6
Survey Forms: Circle 7 (p. 100)
Your Most Wanted (p. 109)
Introducing Jesus Christ (p. 110)

# *Day 1* • Circle 7: Person X

## God's Word for Today

"All authority has been given to Me in heaven and on earth. Go, therefore, and make disciples of all nations, baptizing them in the name of the Father and of the Son and of the Holy Spirit, teaching them to observe everything I have commanded you. And remember, I am with you always, to the end of the age" (Matthew 28:18-20).

 **Read and meditate on "God's Word for Today" (this week's verse to memorize) in the margin and spend a moment in prayer as you begin today's lesson. Remove the Scripture-memory card from the back of your book and begin committing this verse to memory.**

Circle 7 contains Person X. Person X is a stranger, someone you haven't met who needs to know the Lord. This person may briefly cross your path unexpectedly. It may be someone you will never see again but whose salvation you want to continue praying for. Or God may lead you to add someone to this circle whom you know of but have never personally met. You would then begin building a relational bridge.

You may think we have talked about everybody except the lost world out there. But that lost world is all we have been talking about. Why? Because somewhere out there in somebody's circle, your Person X may be listed. You see, your Person X may be in my circle 3. My Person X may be in your circle 2. My world is not your world, and your world is not my world, but if we all put our worlds together, we can reach the whole world!

You will not be able to develop a survey form on Person X in advance. These are more likely to be people who cross your path for the first and perhaps the only time. You must pray and be prepared to love them and meet their needs. Once you have had an experience with a Person X, complete a survey form so that you can remember to pray for that person. Include all the information you know. You may not even know their names, but you can describe them sufficiently to remember how to pray. Who knows? You may cross paths with that person again. God may begin to move a Person X into a closer concentric circle over time.

1) **Have you ever shared your faith with a Person X, someone you had never met before?   ○ Yes   ○ No   If so, how did the experience compare to sharing with someone in your other circles?**

---

Remember when Jesus was walking through the crowds one day? People were jostling Him on every side. Suddenly Jesus turned and asked, "Who touched My robes?" (Mark 5:30). His disciples asked Jesus what He meant since many people were touching Him. But Jesus answered that somebody had really touched Him, and He had felt power leave Him. Then a little woman standing nearby confessed that she had touched him. Through His power she was healed. She was a Person X, and Jesus met her need.

Someone is going to "touch" you. Maybe it will be someone on an airplane like the Hollywood producer I met, someone with a need. It may be someone at the gym or the grocery store. When someone touches you, do they touch God's power? Do they encounter His living water? And will you take the time to meet the needs of that Person X?

People will pass into and out of your life. You may never know when to expect them. But be ready. Pray expectantly for the opportunity to share God's love with Person X. Knowing who needs to be loved, He will bring that unknown person into your circle 7.

② **Are you prepared to meet Person X? Check all that apply.**
   ○ I regularly pray to be ready when I meet Person X.
   ○ I really don't ever think about Person X.
   ○ I ask God to fill me with His Spirit so that I will be prepared to share His love.
   ○ I stay attuned to God's work around me.

Some of my students admit, "You know, when I am walking in submission to my Lord, I bump into more people accidentally who need Jesus than I could ever find on purpose." This happens because God bears fruit in their lives as they become aware of and prepare to meet the needs of Person X.

What is your spiritual temperature? Are you walking closely to the Lord? Do His life and love flow through your life? Does He bring people into your life, knowing they will encounter Christ there?

The Holy Spirit is always resident in a Christian. If you remain filled with the Spirit, He will engineer circumstances to bring Person Xs into your life, knowing that you will be faithful to love them and to meet their needs. In this way you are prepared to reach out to Person Xs, who, like a comet, come into our lives only for a moment and then pass on by. We may never see them again in this lifetime. They may touch us only for a moment. Will they touch power?

③ **Think about the places you frequent where you may encounter Person X. Turn to page 100 and list any people who have passed through your life recently and record any information you have about them.**

**↕ Praying for My Circles Today**

Pray that God will prepare you spiritually to meet Person X. Pray for any Person Xs you listed in circle 7. Pray that God will work in their lives and that you will have another opportunity to meet their needs.

Follow your established plan to pray through your concentric circles.

# Day 2 • Reaching Out Through Circumstances

 **Read and meditate on "God's Word for Today" in the margin and spend a moment in prayer as you begin today's lesson.**

We have learned that one of the best ways to be used by God in reaching your world is to show God's love. Love is meeting needs. As you pray for those in your concentric circles of concern, God will engineer circumstances in the lives of those for whom you are praying so that they will have an opportunity to experience His love through your life. Then as you show God's love and meet their needs, He will begin drawing them to His Son.

Many of our opportunities to share the Lord are blocked and the Spirit of God is quenched because we react wrongly to circumstances. We react as the world reacts, and that does not work in pointing people to the Lord. To avoid missed opportunities, set your attitude in advance by asking yourself, *Who is in control, Jesus or me?* React to circumstances from the attitude that God is in control and that you will allow Him to meet the person's needs through you.

One day as I talked to my class about reacting to circumstances, I said, "God will place you in circumstances in which He wants to love someone through you. If you do not react in agape love—depending on the Holy Spirit, abiding in the Word, and trusting in Him—you will lose your opportunity to share Christ with the person."

After class Jerry came to me and said, "Dr. Thompson, your class is about to plow me under."

I asked, "What's the matter, Jerry?"

He said, "You were talking about God's drawing people into my concentric circles. You said He engineers circumstances to bring people into my life, and the way I respond either gives me the opportunity to share the gospel with them or causes me to lose it."

"That's right," I replied.

Jerry responded, "I think I blew it." Then he told me this story. "I drive my motorbike to work each day. For the past two days as I've pulled into the parking lot, I've noticed a bike exactly like mine, except it doesn't have a mirror. When I came out to the parking lot last night, my mirror was missing. So I walked down to the other bike, and there it was. My mirror was on his bike. I knew it was my mirror because it was marked. I took my mirror off his bike and was so angry that I flooded his bike. It didn't hurt his bike, but it probably took about 30 minutes for him to start it. When I got home, the Lord really began to deal with me. What do I do?"

"Well, I'm not sure, Jerry," I said. "What is the Holy Spirit telling you to do?"

The next week Jerry came back to class and asked to share something with the class. "Friday night I went back to work, and there was this fellow's bike. I thought, I need to treat this fellow as if he were a dear friend who has a need. Apparently, he needs a mirror since he had stolen mine. I went to the store and bought a mirror just like mine and put it on his bike. I also left a note saying, 'I know you stole my mirror. I'm the one who flooded your bike. But because of my relationship with Jesus Christ, He would not tolerate that attitude in my life.' I left the mirror and note with my name and phone number on it.

"That next night the fellow called me. He said, 'I've stolen many things in my life, but I've never received this kind of reaction. Can we talk?' That night in my apartment that guy got down on his knees and gave his life to Jesus."

God leads us, as He did Jerry, into circumstances with family, neighbors, coworkers, and people everywhere you go so that He can reveal Himself through you.

1 **Think of a time when God placed you in an unpleasant circumstance like Jerry's. How did you react?**

○ Like the world    ○ Like a representative of Christ

You never know when Person Xs will show up. The Holy Spirit draws them. They are hungry. They are hurting, but they sense that the world doesn't care. When they come into your life, this may be their only opportunity to hear about God's love. God holds you responsible. He wants you to be available.

If you love everyone in your concentric circles, your life will radiate a holy magnetism. God will draw people through you to him. They may be in your life for only a moment, and you may never see them again, but God puts them there for a purpose. John 7:38 assures that "the one who believes in Me … will have streams of living water flow from deep within him." So if you are walking in the Lord and are in agreement with Him, His living water will flow through your life and touch others.

**Praying for My Circles Today**

Review circle 7 (p. 100) and add any names or information as needed. Does anyone need to be moved to your Most Wanted list (p. 109)? Remember to pray for persons on this list. Watch for ways God is working through you to show love to them or to build deeper relationships with them.

## Day 3 • Missions Awareness

### God's Word for Today
"Then He said to them, 'Go into all the world and preach the gospel to the whole creation'" (Mark 16:15).

### Matthew 28:18-20
"All authority has been given to Me in heaven and on earth. Go, therefore, and make disciples of all nations, baptizing them in the name of the Father and of the Son and of the Holy Spirit, teaching them to observe everything I have commanded you. And remember, I am with you always, to the end of the age."

### Acts 1:8
"You will receive power when the Holy Spirit has come upon you, and you will be My witnesses in Jerusalem, in all Judea and Samaria, and to the ends of the earth."

↕ **Read and meditate on "God's Word for Today" in the margin and spend a moment in prayer as you begin today's lesson.**

For the remainder of our study we will extend our vision to the ends of the earth. Before Jesus ascended to heaven, He gave us our marching orders for reaching the entire world with the gospel of Jesus Christ.

① **Read the Great Commission, Matthew 28:18-20, in the margin. To whom did Jesus command His disciples to take the gospel?**

_____

When Jesus gave us this command, He did not leave out any objects of His love. He commanded us to make disciples of "all nations," or all peoples and ethnic groups. In Mark 16:15 He said, "Go into all the world and preach the gospel to the whole creation." He also gave His followers a wonderful promise.

② **Read Acts 1:8 in the margin. Underline the four areas where Jesus said His followers would be His witnesses.**

Now the assignment is ours. We have his Holy Spirit. We are His witnesses. We must—
- start in Jerusalem (at home, in your city);
- continue into Judea (extended family; surrounding communities, county, state, or province);
- proceed to Samaria (crossing racial, ethnic, and religious barriers);
- continue to the ends of the earth.

The whole world is the object of Jesus' Great Commission: "The Lord does not delay His promise, as some understand delay, but is patient with you, not wanting any to perish, but all to come to repentance" (2 Peter 3:9). We are to carry the gospel to all peoples of all the world. What a humanly impossible assignment! Fortunately, God is always with us, empowering us by His Spirit to carry out the assignment. But we must choose to obey Him. He does not have an alternative plan if we refuse His command.

Jesus didn't issue the Great Commission to an elite corps of super-disciples. He gave the command to a group of ordinary men and to all who would come to faith through their message—that includes you and me. Collectively, we are the body of Christ for our generation. Every Christian and every local congregation of Christians are parts of that larger body of Christ. Every part is needed for the whole body to function as Christ intended. If the whole church (every individual believer in a local congregation and every congregation throughout the world) obeyed Jesus' command, God would make sure the whole world heard the good news about His Son. With God all things are possible.

Because the Great Commission was given to so many, you might be tempted to think your part is so small that it doesn't matter. But every believer and every church has a part to play in this world mission. World-mission assignments are the greatest adventures to be filled in your service to Christ. Whether you stay at home in a support role or go to the front lines of service, you can be a part of God's worldwide mission strategy.

One place to begin is by becoming aware of God's work in other areas. I will use the term *missions* for God's work through the body of Christ to reach a lost world with the gospel of Jesus Christ. This could include home missions (in your country) and international missions (in other countries). When you begin to learn about missions, God may guide you to be involved in specific ways through your support or personal participation.

(3) **Read the following suggestions for developing missions awareness. Check those you are willing to do. Write others in the margin.**

○ Read a missionary's biography. Many missionaries say that they first sensed God's call to missions while reading biographies of missionaries like William Carey, Adoniram Judson, David Brainerd, John "Praying" Hyde, David Livingstone, Jim Elliott, Hudson Taylor, Bertha Smith, Amy Carmichael, William Booth, C. T. Studd, and Lottie Moon.

○ Read about the history of missions in a missions group, a denomination, a parachurch group, a people group, or a country.

○ Watch a video or documentary that tells the story of a missionary or a particular missions effort.

○ Read or listen to news reports and updates from the mission field, as reported in missions magazines, Christian radio, Christian television, newsletters from missionaries, e-mail groups, and Web sites.

○ Attend a missions conference to hear missionaries' reports.

○ Listen to testimonies of people who have been touched by missions.[1]

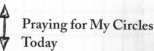

**Praying for My Circles Today**

Pray that God will give you a heart to be on mission to the world.

Pray for your concentric circles according to your plan.

1. Claude King, *Made to Count Life Planner* (Nashville: LifeWay Press, 2004), 116.

## *Day 4* • Missions Support

**God's Word for Today**

"Let us be concerned about one another in order to promote love and good works, not staying away from our meetings, as some habitually do, but encouraging each other, and all the more as you see the day drawing near" (Hebrews 10:24-25).

**Read and meditate on "God's Word for Today" in the margin and spend a moment in prayer as you begin today's lesson.**

Missions awareness prepares you to hear what God may want to do through you. As you become aware of God's activity in a missions area, you can begin to identify ways He is inviting you to join Him in missions support or involvement. Missions support is helping others who are involved in missions work. This is a beginning step in obeying Jesus' Great Commission. Just as Paul received support from churches in the areas of finances, coworkers, and prayers, today's missionaries need the support of other believers.

1. **Read the following suggestions for providing missions support. Check one or more that you are willing to do to provide support for missions work either outside or through your local church.**
   ○ Prayer for missions and missionaries. Pray for—
   - a missionary, his or her family, and his or her work;
   - missionaries on their birthdays;
   - specific requests given by missionaries or organizations;
   - missions organization, administrators, and staff;
   - gateway cities, countries, and areas where missionaries serve;
   - an unreached people group (your church can even adopt one);
   - God to call people to missions involvement;
   - conversion of people in a non-Christian religion;
   - governments and leaders whose laws may grant freedom or hinder missions work in their countries;
   - national leaders (Christian workers in their own country or culture);
   - missions events, crusades, or outreach efforts;
   - use of media like the Jesus film, Gideon Bibles, or Christian radio to reach people for Christ.

   ○ Encouragement. Send letters, cards, e-mails, and gifts that encourage missionaries in their work. Be careful, however, not to let your contacts become a hindrance by taking too much of the missionary's time.

○ Financial support. Obey the Lord's scriptural directions to support missions by giving money to—
  • your church for missions causes;
  • individual missionaries and their projects;
  • organizations that send missionaries;
  • schools that train and equip missionaries for service;
  • emergency requests for disaster relief or hunger projects;
  • volunteers for short- or long-term mission trips;
  • Bible societies or missions radio and television;
  • churches or organizations that support national pastors and missionaries in other countries.

○ Material support. You may have material you can give either from your personal property or through your company, such as medical supplies, food for disaster relief, clothes, blankets, bicycles, cars, Christian books or literature, Bibles, and radio or video equipment. Don't send material, however, without knowing a specific need.

○ Logistical support. Your work or company may be able to provide logistical help for missionaries by coordinating travel, shipping goods, transferring data, providing technical training, and so forth.

○ Your children. Parents and grandparents are sometimes the greatest hindrance to individuals who sense God's call to missions. If your children or grandchildren feel called to missions, give them your blessing. Send them off with your encouragement. Provide all the support at your disposal. Your greatest contribution to Jesus' Great Commission could be godly children who respond to God's call.[1]

2  **What will you do to support missions at home and/or abroad?**

_____

_____

_____

_____

 **Praying for My Circles Today**
Pray about your willingness to support missions. Ask God to show you one or more ways He wants you to support the spread of the gospel.

Examine your Most Wanted list on page 109. Does any information need to be updated? Pray for God's direction in building bridges to your Most Wanted and in sharing His love with them.

1. Claude King, *Made to Count Life Planner* (Nashville: LifeWay Press, 2004), 116–17.

## *Day 5* • Missions Involvement

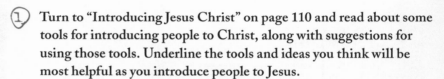

"How can they call on Him in whom they have not believed? And how can they believe without hearing about Him? And how can they hear without a preacher? And how can they preach unless they are sent? As it is written: How welcome are the feet of those who announce the gospel of good things! So faith comes from what is heard, and what is heard comes through the message about Christ" (Romans 10:14-15,17).

 Read and meditate on "God's Word for Today" in the margin and spend a moment in prayer as you begin today's lesson.

Listing people in your surveys and praying for them is a part of the work God uses to point people to Christ. Building relationship bridges and reconciling relationships open the channel through which the gospel and God's love can flow. But people cannot believe in Christ unless someone helps them understand their need and how to repent and believe in Christ. You've already prepared your own testimony of what Christ has done in your life. That is perhaps your most powerful witnessing tool. But what are some other ways you can share the good news about Jesus with your most wanted?

① Turn to "Introducing Jesus Christ" on page 110 and read about some tools for introducing people to Christ, along with suggestions for using those tools. Underline the tools and ideas you think will be most helpful as you introduce people to Jesus.

You can also witness to the world by getting involved in missions and taking the gospel to the ends of the earth in person. You don't have to be a career missionary to get involved in missions. Nearly everyone can become personally involved.

② Read the following suggestions for missions involvement. Check one or more that you are willing to do to be involved in missions work beyond or through your local church.
○ Go as a volunteer on a short-term missions trip. Possibilities include—
  • evangelism projects;
  • Bible distribution;
  • construction projects;
  • medical/dental clinics;
  • discipleship training for people and churches;
  • ministry to missionary children while their parents are involved in meetings or events;
  • music, dramatic presentations (individual or group);
  • community health projects such as drilling water wells, building ponds/reservoirs, and water purification;

- disaster-relief efforts;
- prayerwalking (praying on site with insight), particularly in countries with limited access for missionaries;
- feeding projects;
- teaching business skills or English as a second language;
- ministry to orphans or lepers;
- agricultural projects;
- sports clinics or demonstrations.

○ Minister to people in your area who could carry the gospel home with them. These people might be—
- international students at a university;
- foreign-exchange students;
- international tourists at local attractions;
- international athletes in training or at sports events;
- employees who are temporarily working in your area.

○ If God should call you, go as a career or long-term missionary—
- through your denomination's sending agency;
- through your church or a group of churches;
- for tentmaking (you provide your income through employment while volunteering in missions);
- as part of a parachurch group assignment (you usually raise your support before going and periodically as the need arises).[1]

③ **What will you do to obey Jesus' Great Commission by becoming personally involved in missions? Remember that God is your Master. He calls people to missions. What do you presently sense that God may be calling you to do?**

_____

_____

_____

_____

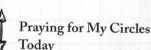

**Praying for My Circles Today**

End your study by praying that God will help you make witnessing to your world your lifestyle. Continue updating and praying through your concentric circles. Surrender your life to be available to God for whatever He asks and wherever He leads.

1. Claude King, *Made to Count Life Planner* (Nashville: LifeWay Press, 2004), 118.

# Leader Guide

If you have not read the introductory remarks on pages 5–7, do so before continuing.

*Witness to the World* is a six-session study in the Growing Disciples Series described on page 112. Although *The Call to Follow Christ* is an introduction to all six disciplines in the series, it is not necessarily a prerequisite. The books in the series can be studied in any sequence; therefore, *Witness to the World* can follow any of the other studies, or it can serve as a starting place for new and growing believers.

This course is designed to teach believers how to witness to the world by reaching out with God's love to the lost people in their circles of influence. As a result of this study, participants will be able to—

- explain how the gospel spreads through relationships;
- evaluate their vertical relationship with God and their horizontal relationships with others in order to be reconciled in all of their relationships;
- identify lost immediate-family members, relatives, friends, neighbors, associates, and acquaintances in their circles of influence who need to know Christ;
- complete survey forms that help them identify the needs of lost people in their concentric circles and ways they can meet those needs;
- intercede in prayer for the lost;
- build relational bridges to lost people;
- reach out with God's love to strangers they encounter;
- identify ways to become involved in God's worldwide redemptive mission.

## Selecting a Leader

Although young believers could study this book together and help one another grow, enlisting a mature believer to lead the group will significantly help the process. Because of the nature of this book's focus on witnessing, an active, experienced witness would be an ideal prospect. Select a leader who has a warm, personal, faithful walk with Christ. Look for good interpersonal skills and the ability to facilitate small-group learning activities.

## Small-Group Study

This resource has been designed for a combination of individual and small-group study. In a small group of other believers, Christians can learn from one another, encourage and strengthen one another, and minister to one another. The body of Christ can function best as members assume responsibility for helping one another grow in Christlikeness. Encourage participants to study the book during the week and then join other believers in the small group to process and apply what they have learned. Provide a separate group for every 8 to 12 participants so that everyone will be able to participate actively.

## One-to-One Mentoring

If circumstances prevent your studying this book in a small-group setting in which you have access to a variety of spiritual gifts, you may choose to use it in a one-to-one mentoring process. To do so, study the lessons each day and meet at least once each week to discuss what you are learning. Use the session plans on pages 83–88 to get ideas for your personal discussions and prayer times.

## Order Books

Each participant will need a copy of this book. Each spouse in a couple will want his or her own book to respond to learning activities and prepare a prayer journal. To order additional copies of this resource, write to LifeWay Church Resources Customer Service; One LifeWay Plaza; Nashville, TN 37234-0113; fax order to (615) 251-5933; phone toll free (800) 458-2772; order online at *www.lifeway.com*; e-mail *orderentry@life-way.com*; or visit a LifeWay Christian Store.

## Enlisting Participants

Any believers who want to obey Jesus' Great Commission will benefit from this study. As you enlist participants, give them a book and ask them to study the introduction and week 1 before the first session. Include mature believers in the group so that each subgroup will include someone who will be comfortable praying for the others and who can lead in discussion and prayer.

## Your Role as the Leader

You are not required to be a content expert to teach this course. Participants study the content during the week. Your role is to facilitate group discussion, sharing, and praying to process and apply what participants have learned during the week. Be sensitive to members' spiritual growth and pay special attention to those who may struggle along the way. Don't hesitate to enlist the help of more mature believers in the group to help you nurture the others and to help facilitate prayer times.

## Time and Schedule

This course is designed for six sessions. Each group session needs to follow the study of the corresponding week's daily devotions. Members will need to have books so that they can study the first week's material prior to the first session. Allow at least one hour for each session. Some groups may prefer longer sessions to accommodate more sharing, discussion, and prayer for one another.

## Preparing to Lead the Sessions

The most important things you can do to prepare for the study each week is to allow the Lord to prepare you and fill you with His Spirit. Make prayer a major part of your preparation throughout the course. God will work and guide in answer to prayer.

Complete the daily lessons and activities just as members are asked to do. Complete your lists of lost people and survey forms as directed so that you will understand what members are experiencing. Seek to build relationships and witness between sessions and be prepared to share your personal experiences during group sessions.

Leading the small-group sessions should not require large amounts of time in advance preparation. However, you will benefit by studying the suggestions on the following pages. Use these as options, not as a rigid structure to follow. Allow the needs of your group to dictate the emphasis you give to each topic. Decide which activities and questions to use in your study and determine approximate times for transitions between segments. Select activities that are most appropriate for your group's maturity level, but don't hesitate to challenge their spiritual growth to new heights.

Provide a marker board and markers for making lists. If members don't already know one another, provide name tags for the first few sessions so that they can easily learn names.

## Leading the Sessions

Select and arrange the activities and discussion questions based on your group's interest and experiences. Adapt the plans to best meet your group's needs. Here are a few ideas for using the sections provided in each session plan.

*Opening prayer and praying together.* Young believers may not be ready to pray aloud in a group. Begin by asking for volunteers. Don't call on people to pray unless you know they could do so comfortably. Give permission for people not to pray aloud until they are ready. Seek to increase their prayer participation as the study progresses. Some prayer suggestions call for members to pray in pairs or in small groups. These times can encourage members to grow in ability and willingness to pray in public.

*Reviewing this week's material.* These activities help you review facts and key ideas from the previous week's daily lessons.

*Interacting with the Scriptures.* This section examines key Scriptures from the week's study and their application to a witnessing lifestyle.

*Connecting with concentric circles.* This focus allows you to make specific application to members' concentric circles of concern. It also serves as a reminder for members to keep their lists and survey forms up-to-date.

Remember, this is a guide that may help you lead your group. But the Holy Spirit is your true Guide. Allow Him to show you what questions to ask and the direction He wants the group to take each week.

**Opening Prayer**

**Reviewing Week 1**

1. Ask: *Why should a Christian have a personal strategy for reaching his or her world?*
2. Discuss examples from your own experiences of how a Christian's lifestyle has had a positive or negative influence on others' coming to Christ.
3. Invite volunteers to tell how they came to a saving relationship with Jesus Christ. Ask: *Who was the person most responsible for helping you come to Christ, and what was that person's relationship to you?*
4. Ask: *How have you experienced God working through a relationship to bring a person to faith in Christ?*
5. Direct attention to "Preparing Your Story" on page 102. Point out the importance of being prepared to share a testimony when the opportunity arises.
6. Ask: *What have you done or experienced in the past week as a result of our study so far? How is God working in your relationships?*
7. Ask: *What do you sense is the most meaningful or valuable truth God is teaching you about concentric circles of concern?*

**Interacting with the Scriptures**

1. Read Acts 1:8. Ask members to identify the four areas in which we are to be witnesses. Explain how the gospel spreads through relationships in ever-widening circles.
2. Referring to the examples in day 3, ask: *In the New Testament how did the gospel move in the context of relationships?*

**Connecting with Concentric Circles**

1. Have members turn to the concentric-circles diagram on page 89. Explain the meaning of each circle. Point out that members should have listed their immediate-family members and relatives this week.
2. Ask each member to think of one person in his or her concentric circles who needs to know Christ as Savior.

**Praying Together**

Ask each member: *How may we pray for you this week?* Ask members to form small groups and to pray specifically for one another and for the persons in their lives who need Christ.

# Session 2 • The Importance of Healthy Relationships

**Opening Prayer**

**Reviewing Week 2**

1. Suppose you met a lost person who asked you, "What are God's conditions for me to come to Him?" What would you say?
2. Invite volunteers to share one or more of the following:
   - One of my most joyful and happy experiences growing up was ...
   - One of my most significant positive relationships with another person is (or was) ...
   - One of the darkest, saddest times in my past was ...
3. Discuss ways your home life growing up has affected your successes or failures in relationships. Ask: *What are positive lessons you learned about relationships?*
4. Ask members what insights they gained by completing "Your Horizontal Relationships with Others" on pages 104–5.
5. Discuss ways your church experience has (or could) provided a divine hospital for healing relationships.
6. Invite volunteers to describe a relationship that needs to be reconciled.
7. Ask: *How has God guided you to reconcile with another person? What did you do? How did the other person respond?*
8. Ask: *In what broken relationship are you still struggling to seek reconciliation? How may we pray for you in this relationship? What can we do to help you?* Discuss ways you can help one another get relationships right.

9. Ask: *What have you done or experienced in the past week as a result of our study so far? How is God working in your relationships?*

**Interacting with the Scriptures**
Read Matthew 5:23-24. Ask: *What did Jesus say we are to do to right broken relationships?*

**Connecting with Concentric Circles**
Remind members to continually revisit their survey forms to add information and to pray through their lists.

**Praying Together**
Ask each member: *How may we pray for you this week?* Pray for members' requests as well as the following concerns.
- Thanksgiving for meaningful relationships of the past
- Spiritual healing for brokenness from past relationships
- Current relationships that need to be reconciled
- Current relationships that call for a demonstration of love by meeting needs
- Members' obedience in seeking to reconcile relationships
- People you sense God wants to love into the Kingdom through your life

## Opening Prayer

## Reviewing Week 3

1. Ask volunteers to relate experiences when they were not in a right relationship with God. Ask: *What were the circumstances? How did God reveal your need to get right with Him? How did you respond to Him?*

2. Ask members to describe times when they felt and experienced a close personal relationship with their Heavenly Father. Ask: *What are some ways you experience that closeness on a regular basis?*

3. Ask volunteers to share any insights from their completion of "Your Vertical Relationship with God" on pages 106–7.

4. Read James 5:16. Ask members to confess to a partner ways they hurt or feel bad about themselves and to state how those feelings have caused them to act in ways that are displeasing to the Lord.

5. Ask volunteers to share ways God is leading them to bring problems and insecurities to Him.

6. Ask: *What are some ways God can work through Christians to encourage and build one another up?* List these on the board. Challenge members to support their fellow believers in these ways.

7. Ask: *What have you done or experienced in the past week as a result of our study so far? How is God working in your relationships?*

## Interacting with the Scriptures

Read John 7:38. Ask: *What does it mean to have stream of living water flowing through you?*

## Connecting with Concentric Circles

1. State that members should have focused on self and immediate family this week. Remind them that they should have added information to their survey forms as they prayed for family members.

2. Ask: *What special insights have you gained about the members of your immediate family? Have you prayed in a special way for them that has proved to be especially meaningful? How?*

3. Ask: *What are some ways God has led you to meet the needs of family members, and how have they responded? Has love returned to you in a special way?*

## Praying Together

1. Ask each member: *How may we pray for you this week?* Ask members to pray with the partners they talked with earlier—for emotional and spiritual healing, conformity to God's will for their lives, and God's power to end destructive behavior.

2. Pray for the specific needs of any family members who have been mentioned. Also pray for members' relationships with and witness to immediate-family members.

# Session 4 • Concentric Circles 3–6: Relatives, Friends, Neighbors, Associates, and Acquaintances

## Opening Prayer

## Reviewing Week 4

1. Ask members to name reasons it is important to keep their survey forms up-to-date (see p. 46).
2. Ask: *What relatives, friends, neighbors, associates, and acquaintances have you added to your survey forms who seemed to surface unexpectedly? Have you experienced any unusual circumstances this week that seemed to heighten your awareness of their needs?*
3. Explain that we are designed for God's love to flow through us to others. Ask whether members have broken relationships with anyone they have listed this week or whether anyone on their lists is a problem person. Ask: *How may we pray with and for you about that relationship?*
4. Ask: *What unique, unusual, or especially meaningful experiences have you had this week as you have prayed for and reached out to the people in your concentric circles?*
5. Review "God's Activity Watch List" on page 108. Ask: *In what ways have you seen God begin to answer some of your prayers since you began this study?* Urge members to remain sensitive to God's activity in the lives of those for whom they are praying.
6. Ask: *What have you done or experienced in the past week as a result of our study so far? How is God working in your relationships?*

## Interacting with the Scriptures

1. Read John 15:12. Ask: *How can we show God's love to others?*

2. Ask volunteers to read John 14:6; Acts 4:12; and 1 John 5:12. Explain that without Christ our relatives, friends, neighbors, associates, and acquaintances are condemned to hell. Stress the urgency of sharing Christ now.

## Connecting with Concentric Circles

1. Direct attention to the circles on page 89 and explain the meaning of each circle. Remind members that they should have completed survey forms on relatives, friends, neighbors, associates, and acquaintances this week.
2. Ask: *What special insights have you gained about your relatives, friends, neighbors, associates, and acquaintances? Have you prayed in a special way for them that has proved to be especially meaningful? How?*
3. Ask: *What are some ways God has led you to meet needs, and how have people responded? Has love returned to you in a special way?*
4. Direct attention to "Introducing Jesus Christ" on page 110. This Discipleship Help will be used in week 6, but members may want to begin using some of these tools or ideas as they share Christ with people.

## Praying Together

Ask each member: *How may we pray for you this week?* Pray for the broken relationships or problem people mentioned earlier and for members' efforts to reach out to their relatives, friends, neighbors, associates, and acquaintances.

## Opening Prayer

## Reviewing Week 5

1. Ask: *Why is intercession important in reaching the lost for Christ? What breakthroughs have you seen in reaching the lost since you started interceding for your concentric circles? How has your prayer life changed?*
2. Ask: *Based on your experiences, what are the greatest barriers to your sharing the gospel with others? How have you experienced God's help in overcoming those barriers?*
3. Ask: *What are barriers to our church's sharing the gospel? What can we do to remove those barriers so that the gospel will flow freely through our members to the lost world?*
4. Draw attention to the ideas for building bridges in days 3–4. Ask: *What are some ways you have built relational bridges with lost people since beginning this study?*
5. Ask: *How can you build relational bridges to people in your circles and with whom?*
6. Ask members to describe instances in which they experienced God's love through others who met their needs. Ask: *What did they do? How did you respond?*
7. Ask: *What are some ways God is teaching you to show love by meeting the needs of others?*
8. Ask: *Are you struggling with the idea of meeting needs in any way?* Discuss. Remind members that we must love our enemies and the unlovely. Consider ways to overcome these difficulties.
9. Discuss how God want us to respond when our love is not returned. Ask: *What did Jesus do when His love wasn't returned?*
10. Ask: *What have you done or experienced in the past week as a result of our study so far? How is God working in your relationships?*

## Interacting with the Scriptures

1. Read James 1:5; 4:2. Ask: *Why is it important to pray specifically?* Ask participants to share their experiences using the prayer pattern suggested on pages 60–61.
2. Read 1 Corinthians 9:19-22. Ask: *How did Paul build relationships to bring others to Christ?*
3. Read Matthew 25:35-40. Ask: *How does meeting needs show love to God?*

## Connecting with Concentric Circles

1. Ask volunteers to share their plans for praying through their concentric circles on a regular basis (p. 59).
2. Ask to to tell about the persons they added to their Most Wanted list (p. 61). Challenge members to build relational bridges to these and others on their lists.

## Praying Together

Ask each member: *How may we pray for you this week?* Ask members to pray in small groups—

- for their Most Wanted;
- for opportunities to build relationships with the lost and to meet their needs;
- for their attitudes toward their enemies and the unlovely on their lists;
- for the Lord to engineer circumstances to draw people in their lives to Him.

**Opening Prayer**

**Reviewing Week 6**

1. Ask: *What can we do to remain prepared to meet Person X?* State that the key is walking closely with the Lord and continually being filled with His Spirit.

2. Ask: *What are some times or ways you have blown it in building relational bridges? How do you think you could have done things differently to show God's love?* Emphasize the importance of being prepared to witness of Christ even in negative circumstances. Challenge members to live in a way that draws the lost to Jesus.

3. Ask volunteers to share ways they would like to increase their missions awareness (p. 75), their missions support (pp. 76–77), and their missions involvement (pp. 78–79). Add opportunities that are available through your church or denomination.

4. Ask: *In what ways has this study prepared you to share the gospel with others? How have you already presented the gospel to other people? How have they responded?*

5. Discuss whether your church is a come-and-listen church or a tell-as-you-go church. Ask: *What can we do to be more a tell-as-you-go church?*

6. Ask: *What has God done in you or in the lives of others during this study that has had the greatest impact for His kingdom?*

**Interacting with the Scriptures**

1. Read Matthew 28:18-29 and Acts 1:8. Ask members to define our worldwide mission assignment, as explained in day 3.

**Connecting with Concentric Circles**

1. Define Person X. Ask: *How can someone's concentric circles sometimes intersect with those of others (p. 70)?*

2. Challenge members to keep praying through and updating their concentric circles according to the plan they established in week 5. Remind them to move names to their Most Wanted list as the Lord leads.

3. Provide samples of some of the witnessing tools listed on page 110. Discuss ways group members plan to introduce people in their circles to Jesus Christ.

**Praying Together**

1. Ask each member: *How may we pray for you in the coming weeks?* Ask members to pray in pairs for their each other's needs, for their Most Wanted, and for God's guidance in identifying their next steps in reaching them.

2. Close by thanking God for what He has taught the group and what He has done in and through your lives. Ask Him to empower and give wisdom to members as they work to build relationships and reach their world for Christ.

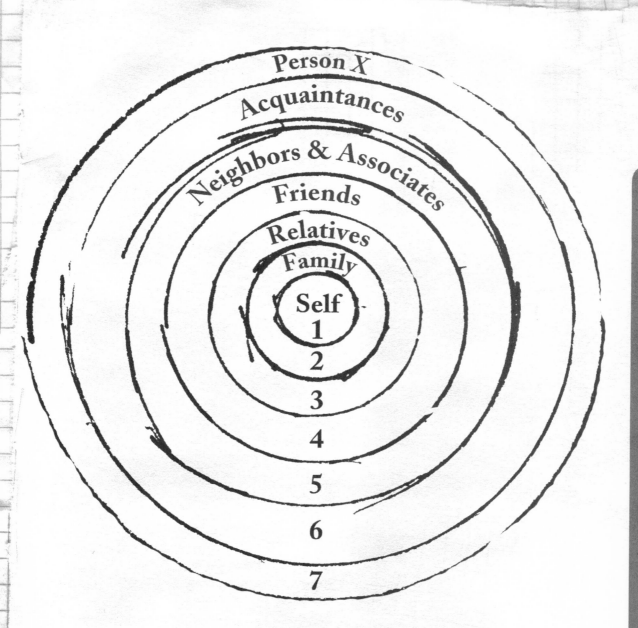

Person X
Acquaintances
Neighbors & Associates
Friends
Relatives
Family
Self
1
2
3
4
5
6
7

# Circle 2: Immediate Family

Your immediate family includes those who live under your roof. If you are away from home and are not married, your survey for circle 2 will include your mother and father. If you are married, your immediate family will be your spouse and children. The rest of your family will go in circle 3, relatives.

List the people in your immediate family. Include the following.
- Husband or wife _____
- Mother and father _____
- Stepparents _____
- Children _____
  _____
- Stepchildren _____
  _____
- Others in your household _____
  _____
  _____

## SURVEY FORM

Name _____
Address _____
City, state, ZIP _____
Home phone _____ Work phone _____
Cell phone_____ Relationship _____
   ○ Single   ○ Married   ○ Divorced   ○ Widowed   ○ Separated
Prayer requests/needs/circumstances _____
_____
Birthday _____ Anniversary_____
Occupation/place of employment _____
Hobbies/interests _____
Times of joy or stress to remember and date _____
Strategy _____
Date gospel presented _____
Response _____
_____

## SURVEY FORM

Name _____

Address _____

City, state, ZIP _____

Home phone _____ Work phone _____

Cell phone_____ Relationship _____

    ○ Single   ○ Married   ○ Divorced   ○ Widowed   ○ Separated

Prayer requests/needs/circumstances _____

_____

Birthday _____ Anniversary _____

Occupation/place of employment _____

Hobbies/interests _____

Times of joy or stress to remember and date _____

Strategy _____

Date gospel presented _____

Response _____

---

## SURVEY FORM

Name _____

Address _____

City, state, ZIP _____

Home phone _____ Work phone _____

Cell phone_____ Relationship _____

    ○ Single   ○ Married   ○ Divorced   ○ Widowed   ○ Separated

Prayer requests/needs/circumstances _____

_____

Birthday _____ Anniversary _____

Occupation/place of employment _____

Hobbies/interests _____

Times of joy or stress to remember and date _____

Strategy _____

Date gospel presented _____

Response _____

## Circle 3: Relatives

List relatives by blood or marriage. Include the following.
- Grandchildren _____
  _____
  _____

- Sisters and brothers _____
  _____

- Grandparents _____
- Aunts and uncles _____
  _____

- Cousins _____
  _____

- Nieces and nephews _____
  _____
  _____

- In-laws_____

---

## SURVEY FORM

Name _____

Address _____

City, state, ZIP _____

Home phone _____ Work phone _____

Cell phone_____ Relationship _____

○ Single   ○ Married   ○ Divorced   ○ Widowed   ○ Separated

Prayer requests/needs/circumstances _____

_____

Birthday _____ Anniversary _____

Occupation/place of employment _____

Hobbies/interests _____

Times of joy or stress to remember and date _____

Strategy _____

Date gospel presented _____

Response _____

_____

## SURVEY FORM

Name _____

Address _____

City, state, ZIP _____

Home phone _____ Work phone _____

Cell phone _____ Relationship _____

○ Single ○ Married ○ Divorced ○ Widowed ○ Separated

Prayer requests/needs/circumstances _____

_____

Birthday _____ Anniversary _____

Occupation/place of employment _____

Hobbies/interests _____

Times of joy or stress to remember and date _____

Strategy _____

Date gospel presented _____

Response _____

_____

## SURVEY FORM

Name _____

Address _____

City, state, ZIP _____

Home phone _____ Work phone _____

Cell phone _____ Relationship _____

○ Single ○ Married ○ Divorced ○ Widowed ○ Separated

Prayer requests/needs/circumstances _____

_____

Birthday _____ Anniversary _____

Occupation/place of employment _____

Hobbies/interests _____

Times of joy or stress to remember and date _____

Strategy _____

Date gospel presented _____

Response _____

_____

## Circle 4: Friends

List the names of people to whom you are particularly close—those you spend time with, care about, trust for counsel, confide in, or depend on in times of need. If you are close to the friend's family, include the names of family members as well. Include in-town friends and out-of-town friends. You may even want to include friends from your past whom you cared about deeply, even though you do not currently maintain contact.

_____    _____
_____    _____
_____    _____
_____    _____
_____    _____
_____    _____
_____    _____
_____    _____
_____    _____

### SURVEY FORM

Name _____

Address _____

City, state, ZIP _____

Home phone _____  Work phone _____

Cell phone_____  Relationship _____

○ Single  ○ Married  ○ Divorced  ○ Widowed  ○ Separated

Prayer requests/needs/circumstances _____

_____

Birthday _____  Anniversary _____

Occupation/place of employment _____

Hobbies/interests _____

Times of joy or stress to remember and date _____

Strategy _____

Date gospel presented _____

Response _____

_____

## SURVEY FORM

Name _____

Address _____

City, state, ZIP _____

Home phone _____ Work phone _____

Cell phone_____ Relationship _____

      ○ Single  ○ Married  ○ Divorced  ○ Widowed  ○ Separated

Prayer requests/needs/circumstances _____

_____

Birthday _____ Anniversary _____

Occupation/place of employment _____

Hobbies/interests _____

Times of joy or stress to remember and date _____

Strategy _____

Date gospel presented _____

Response _____

_____

## SURVEY FORM

Name _____

Address _____

City, state, ZIP _____

Home phone _____ Work phone _____

Cell phone_____ Relationship _____

      ○ Single  ○ Married  ○ Divorced  ○ Widowed  ○ Separated

Prayer requests/needs/circumstances _____

_____

Birthday _____ Anniversary _____

Occupation/place of employment _____

Hobbies/interests _____

Times of joy or stress to remember and date _____

Strategy _____

Date gospel presented _____

Response _____

_____

# Circle 5: Neighbors and Associates

List neighbors who live near you on your street, in your neighborhood, in your apartment building or complex, in your dorm, and so forth. You may need to do research to discover the names of those who live near you. The Lighthouses of Prayer movement suggests that you begin praying for 5 families on your left, 5 on your right, and 11 across the street.

_____     _____
_____     _____
_____     _____
_____     _____
_____     _____
_____     _____
_____     _____
_____     _____

Also list the names of your coworkers and associates—those you regularly see and interact with while performing your work duties. Include the following.

- Coworkers _____

_____

- Students you teach _____
- Supervisors/management _____
- Teammates in sports or recreational activities _____
- Subordinates _____
- Fellow club members _____
- Clients _____

_____

- Fellow volunteers with whom you regularly work _____

_____

- Vendors _____
- Accountants/bookkeepers _____
- Other employees in your workplace _____

_____

- Attorneys _____
- Fellow union members _____
- Other professionals with whom you work _____
- School classmates and teachers _____

_____

## SURVEY FORM

Name _____

Address _____

City, state, ZIP _____

Home phone _____ Work phone _____

Cell phone _____ Relationship _____

○ Single ○ Married ○ Divorced ○ Widowed ○ Separated

Prayer requests/needs/circumstances _____

_____

Birthday _____ Anniversary _____

Occupation/place of employment _____

Hobbies/interests _____

Times of joy or stress to remember and date _____

Strategy _____

Date gospel presented _____

Response _____

_____

## SURVEY FORM

Name _____

Address _____

City, state, ZIP _____

Home phone _____ Work phone _____

Cell phone _____ Relationship _____

○ Single ○ Married ○ Divorced ○ Widowed ○ Separated

Prayer requests/needs/circumstances _____

_____

Birthday _____ Anniversary _____

Occupation/place of employment _____

Hobbies/interests _____

Times of joy or stress to remember and date _____

Strategy _____

Date gospel presented _____

Response _____

_____

# Circle 6: Acquaintances

List the names of people you see only occasionally or for short periods. You may not know these people well, but you know their names or their faces. Include people you know from places like the following.

- Grocery or department store _____
- Library _____
- Gas station/market _____
- Barbershop/hair salon _____
- Doctor's/dentist's office _____
- Mall _____
- Restaurant _____
- Fitness center/gym _____
- Businesses you frequent _____
- School _____
- Public transportation _____
- Government offices _____

## SURVEY FORM

Name _____
Address _____
City, state, ZIP _____
Home phone _____ Work phone _____
Cell phone _____ Relationship _____
  ○ Single  ○ Married  ○ Divorced  ○ Widowed  ○ Separated
Prayer requests/needs/circumstances _____
_____
Birthday _____ Anniversary _____
Occupation/place of employment _____
Hobbies/interests _____
Times of joy or stress to remember and date _____
Strategy _____
Date gospel presented _____
Response _____
_____

## SURVEY FORM

Name _____

Address _____

City, state, ZIP _____

Home phone _____ Work phone _____

Cell phone_____ Relationship _____

    ○ Single  ○ Married  ○ Divorced  ○ Widowed  ○ Separated

Prayer requests/needs/circumstances _____

_____

Birthday _____ Anniversary _____

Occupation/place of employment _____

Hobbies/interests _____

Times of joy or stress to remember and date _____

Strategy _____

Date gospel presented _____

Response _____

_____

## SURVEY FORM

Name _____

Address _____

City, state, ZIP _____

Home phone _____ Work phone _____

Cell phone_____ Relationship _____

    ○ Single  ○ Married  ○ Divorced  ○ Widowed  ○ Separated

Prayer requests/needs/circumstances _____

_____

Birthday _____ Anniversary _____

Occupation/place of employment _____

Hobbies/interests _____

Times of joy or stress to remember and date _____

Strategy _____

Date gospel presented _____

Response _____

_____

# Circle 7: Person X

Person X is someone you don't know personally but for whom God gives you a special prayer concern. This list can also include persons you once met in passing and may never see again. These may be people who live either in your town or a long distance from you. Think of the following people you may have encountered.

- Civic or government leader _____
- Coach or athlete _____
- Schoolteacher or principal _____
- Someone in the news _____
- Business person/leader _____
- Law-enforcement officer _____
- Business owner you see in commercials _____
- Public servant/employee _____
- Media personality _____
- Entertainer _____
- Homeless persons _____

## SURVEY FORM

Name _____

Address _____

City, state, ZIP _____

Home phone _____ Work phone _____

Cell phone _____ Relationship _____

○ Single  ○ Married  ○ Divorced  ○ Widowed  ○ Separated

Prayer requests/needs/circumstances _____

_____

Birthday _____ Anniversary _____

Occupation/place of employment _____

Hobbies/interests _____

Times of joy or stress to remember and date _____

Strategy _____

Date gospel presented _____

Response _____

_____

# *Praying for Those Yet to Believe*

Use this tool to pray for the people you want to come to Christ. Read the following suggestions for ways to ask God to work in each person's life. Check those that are meaningful or applicable to the person's circumstances.

○ Bring the person to recognize and understand his emptiness and purposelessness in life. Bring him to the end of himself so that he will turn to You.

○ Cause him to hunger and thirst for more in life.

○ Bring him to understand the truth of his condition without Christ and to understand what Christ has done to make his salvation possible.

○ Bring conviction of sin. Allow the consequences of his sin to cause him to desire a different life. Let him become disgusted with his life as it is.

○ Jesus, reveal the Father to him.

○ Father, exalt Jesus in his eyes.

○ Father, draw him to Yourself and to Your Son Jesus.

○ Guide and create circumstances that create a need. Then show Your love by meeting needs through me or other Christ-followers.

○ Bring godly people into his life that will influence him for Christ.

○ Prepare circumstances in his relationships so that another Christian or I will have the opportunity to forgive him and thus reveal Your mercy.

○ Open his ears to hear Your call.

○ Allow him to see the unity and love of Your people in a way that convinces him that Jesus must be sent from You. Convince him that Jesus is indeed the Savior of the world.

○ Prepare his life to receive the planting of Your Word.

○ Protect him from Satan's attempts to blind him and steal the Word that has been sown.

○ Reduce the cares of the world around him that could choke the planted seed.

○ Raise up intercessors in behalf of this person. Guide my prayers for him.

○ Reveal to me the time and the way for me to share a witness about You and the good news of salvation.

○ Bring him under the hearing and influence of Your Word through teaching or preaching. Create in him an openness to listen.

○ Create opportunities for him to hear a witness for Christ from several different trusted sources. Use the timing and diversity of these witnesses to convince him that You are the Author behind them all.

○ Cause him to recognize his need for a Savior.

○ Lord, do whatever it takes to cause this person to seek You. Break the hardness of his heart toward You.

Claude King, *Final Command Action Manual* (Murfreesboro, TN: Final Command Resources, 2001), 49–50.

# Preparing Your Story

A witness is someone who testifies to what he or she has heard, seen, learned, or experienced. Your account of the way you placed your faith in Jesus Christ is a powerful tool because it is true. As you allow Christ's life to show through your life, God can use your testimony to convince others of their need for a relationship with Christ. Use these suggestions to prepare your testimony.

## IDENTIFY WITH SOMEONE IN SCRIPTURE WHO MET JESUS

Consider beginning your story with a brief example of a person in Scripture who came to faith in Jesus Christ.

1. Timothy grew up in a godly home with religious instruction prior to coming to faith in Christ (see 2 Timothy 1:5).
2. The Samaritan woman at the well had been through five failed relationships before recognizing that she needed a relationship with Jesus Christ, the Living Water (see John 4:7-42).
3. Zacchaeus was an influential but disrespected tax collector who responded to Jesus' invitation and changed his lifestyle (see Luke 19:1-10).
4. The demon-possessed man was out of control and in spiritual bondage until Jesus set him free (see Mark 5:1-20).
5. Thomas overcame doubts to follow Christ (see John 20:24-31).
6. Saul of Tarsus opposed Christianity until meeting Jesus and becoming a powerful preacher of the good news (see Acts 9:1-31).
7. Lydia was a businesswoman who was transformed when she came to know the truth about Christ (see Acts 16:13-15).
8. The Philippian jailer, at a time of crisis when his life could have been at stake, heard and believed the good news about Jesus (see Acts 16:16-34).

## REVIEW YOUR EXPERIENCE WITH CHRIST

What have you experienced of life in Christ that would prompt someone else to want to know Him? What about your story could others identify with? With what need in your past might they identify? What in your life with Christ would they desire? Why would they want to know the Jesus Christ you have come to know? Consider these questions.

1. What was your life like before you met Christ?
2. What caused you to recognize your need for a Savior?
3. How did you learn about Jesus and the way you could receive His gift of eternal life?
4. What were your greatest challenges in choosing to follow Christ?
5. Who was the most influential person in pointing you to Jesus?
6. When and how did you choose to turn to Christ and follow Him? What Scriptures played a part in your decision?
7. What difference has Christ made in your life?
8. Why would you recommend that others meet Jesus Christ?

## WRITE YOUR STORY

Use the lines below to write a beginning draft of your story. Don't glorify your past without Christ. Give the greatest focus to the difference Christ has made or the fullness of your life now because of Him. Refine your story so that you can tell others what Jesus means to you.

_____

_____

_____

_____

_____

_____

_____

_____

_____

_____

_____

_____

_____

_____

_____

_____

_____

_____

_____

_____

_____

_____

_____

_____

_____

_____

_____

_____

Claude King, *Made to Count Life Planner* (Nashville: LifeWay Press, 2004), 202.

# Your Horizontal Relationships with Others

Check any relationship in your life that needs reconciliation. If you wish, write a name or initials in the margin as a reminder of a relationship that needs to be made right.

○ Have I mistreated anyone by my actions or words?

○ Have I stolen from a person, an organization, a business, my employer, or anyone else?

○ Do I hold a grudge or bitterness in my heart toward anyone?

○ Have I gossiped about or slandered someone?

○ Have I borrowed anything I have failed to return?

○ Has God led me to do something to meet someone's needs, and I have failed to obey?

○ Have I done anything illegal I need to confess?

○ Have I lied to anyone or falsified information?

○ Have I hurt someone because of an immoral act and covered it up?

○ Am I in a wrong or immoral relationship?

○ Have I been guilty of not expressing gratitude to a person or group when I should have?

○ Am I taking someone for granted and need to show my gratitude in words and deeds?

○ Have I allowed jealously, envy, or resentment to have a negative effect on the way I have related to a person or group?

○ Have I allowed pride to keep me from relating to a person who needed a friend?

○ Have I sinned against God and another person or group by committing any of the following sins?

| | | | | |
|---|---|---|---|---|
| ○ Anger | ○ Anxiety | ○ Arguing | ○ Arrogance | ○ Bitterness |
| ○ Blasphemy | ○ Boasting | ○ Coarse talking | ○ Conceit | ○ Complaining |
| ○ Competition | ○ Controlling spirit | ○ Covetousness | ○ Cursing | ○ Critical spirit |
| ○ Deception | ○ Discord | ○ Disorder | ○ Divisiveness | ○ Envy |
| ○ Factions | ○ Faultfinding | ○ Fear | ○ Fits of rage | ○ Gossip |
| ○ Greed | ○ Grumbling | ○ Hatred | ○ Hypocrisy | ○ Impatience |
| ○ Impurity | ○ Independence | ○ Injustice | ○ Insensitivity | ○ Jealousy |
| ○ Lack of love | ○ Lies | ○ Malice | ○ Oppression | ○ Persecution |
| ○ Prejudice | ○ Pride | ○ Quarreling | ○ Resentment | ○ Revenge |
| ○ Rudeness | ○ Slander | ○ Stereotyping | ○ Strife | ○ Self-seeking |
| ○ Judgmental spirit | ○ Intolerance of differences | ○ Lawsuits among believers | ○ Keeping a record of wrongs | ○ Provoking one another |
| ○ Self-centeredness | ○ Struggle for control | ○ Spirit of superiority | ○ Unforgiveness | ○ Unbelief |
| ○ Selfish ambition | | | | |
| ○ Delighting in a brother's downfall | | | | |

If the Holy Spirit has brought to your mind any relationships that are broken, decide now to make those relationships right. List any persons or groups whom you have offended by your sin and need to be forgiven and reconciled.

_____

_____

Perhaps others have sinned against you. Have you forgiven them as Jesus has commanded? If you hold a grudge, bitterness, ill will, or hatred toward a person, you probably have not forgiven.

List any persons or groups who have offended you or sinned against you whom you have not yet forgiven. If you have a question about whether you have forgiven, add the person's name to your list anyway.

_____

_____

If you have listed persons or groups on the previous lines, you need to reconcile the broken relationship. Use these suggestions to respond to those on your lists.

## IF YOU ARE THE OFFENDER

1. Pray and ask God for help in thorough repentance.
2. Go make things right in obedience to God.
3. Go to the most difficult person first.
4. Confess your sin to God and to those directly affected by the sin.
5. Don't apologize. Ask for forgiveness.
6. Go in person (best choice), call by phone (second choice), or write a letter (last resort).
7. Don't reflect negatively on the other person or his actions or attitudes. Deal only with your part of the offense.
8. Make restitution (pay for the offense) when appropriate.
9. Don't expect to receive a positive response every time. Continue to pray for and seek reconciliation with an unforgiving person. Jesus' command is "Be reconciled."[1]

## IF YOU ARE THE ONE OFFENDED

1. Forgive the offender. Forgiveness is a command, not an option (see Matt. 6:15; Col. 3:13).
2. You cannot forgive and love in your own strength. The Holy Spirit of Christ in you can enable you to forgive and love. Ask Him to enable you to forgive.
3. Forgiveness is a choice of your will, not a feeling. You must choose to forgive.
4. Begin to pray for God to work in the person's life for his or her good. Continue praying until you can do so with a sincere desire to see God bless the person.
5. Make an investment in the person who wronged you by returning good for evil.

Ask God to guide you in this response and in its timing. Ask God what you can do to meet a need or to show love.[2]

## TEACHINGS ON FORGIVENESS

1. Forgiveness is fully releasing another from the debt of the offense.
2. The person who forgives is the one who has to pay the price of forgiveness, just as Jesus paid the price for you.
3. You are never more like Jesus than when you forgive and show grace and mercy. Being offended provides you with the invitation to reveal Christ to the offender by your forgiveness.
4. Forgiveness does not mean the offense was not wrong.
5. Forgiveness is not permission for the offender to do it again. It does not require you to place yourself in harm's way again.
6. Forgiveness does not mean you will fully forget. However, you choose not to hold the offense against the person any longer.
7. How much do you forgive? Jesus said, "70 times seven" (Matt. 18:22). In other words, forgive an unlimited number of times.
8. Jesus said, "If [your brother] sins against you seven times in a day, and comes back to you seven times, saying, 'I repent,' you must forgive him" (Luke 17:4). In other words, even if the offender really doesn't repent and change his ways, you should still forgive.
9. Even if the person doesn't believe he is wrong, forgive. Jesus set the model for us on the cross when He prayed for those who were killing Him (see Luke 23:34).[3]

---

1. Claude King, *Come to the Lord's Table* (Nashville: LifeWay Press, 2006), 70.
2. Ibid., 72–73.
3. Ibid., 72.

# Your Vertical Relationship with God

Prayerfully read the following list of sins and areas of sin. Ask the Lord to reveal to you any area in which you have not turned away from sin and experienced His cleansing. Ask Him to show you any sin that hinders your fellowship with Him. You may want to check any God identifies so that you can seriously deal with your sin. You may prefer to write these on a separate sheet of paper that can be disposed of later.

- ○ Unbelief—not believing God will keep His word
- ○ Rebellion—disobedience, not letting Christ be Lord of all, living my own way
- ○ Pride/arrogance—thinking more highly of myself than I ought
- ○ Bitterness, unforgiveness, holding a grudge
- ○ Sins of the tongue—gossip, slander, murmuring, lying, cursing, filthy speech, vain talk, obscenity
- ○ Dishonesty, deceit
- ○ Mental impurity
- ○ Addiction to harmful or illegal substances
- ○ Addiction to pornography (either visual or written)
- ○ Sexual immorality
- ○ Stealing, cheating, embezzlement
- ○ Anger, hatred, malice, rage, uncontrolled temper
- ○ Idolatry—worshiping another god or loving something or someone more than I love God
- ○ Poor stewardship of my time and resources
- ○ Prayerlessness
- ○ Taking unfair advantage of others, oppressing others
- ○ Disobedience to the Lord's clear commands
- ○ Injustice, failing to defend the oppressed
- ○ Murder, hating others without a cause
- ○ Causing strife, conflict, and dissension in the church
- ○ Worshiping with my lips when my heart is far away from loving the Lord
- ○ Leaving my first love for Christ by loving other people, things, or activities more than the Lord
- ○ Others: _____
  _____
  _____
  _____
  _____
  _____
  _____
  _____
  _____

This is certainly not a complete list of sins. You can miss God's standards in many ways through your thoughts, actions, and words. Develop a heart that is ready to confess and repent at the slightest whisper of conviction from the Holy Spirit. If God has convicted you of sin, take these actions now to get right with Him.

1. Confess: agree with God that you have sinned.
2. Repent: turn away from your sin and turn to God to live His way.
3. Seek the Lord's forgiveness and cleansing.
4. Show your repentance by a changed life/ deeds.[1]

Now ask the Lord to reveal any idols of the heart that may have led you away from your wholehearted love for the Lord. Idols can be things, relationships, or activities. They may not be evil in themselves, but perhaps they have captured too much of your love. One way to test something is to ask yourself, *If God asked me to give this up, would I resist Him or struggle to obey?* If you are holding on too tightly, the item may be an idol of the heart. Only the Lord can reveal to you whether something has captured your love, but He will if you ask Him. Examples could include—

- hobbies or collections;
- a material object you treasure too dearly;
- material things that consume far too much of your time using them or maintaining them;
- things that you own to impress others or that cause you to feel arrogant or condescending toward others;
- things you have purchased for yourself that you know God didn't want you to have;
- activities you love that consume too much of your time and may keep you from your time with God or from obediently serving Him (like television, sports, work/career, or recreation);
- relationships that keep you from your first love for Christ.

List things or activities God brings to your mind. Use extra paper if you need more space.

_____
_____
_____
_____
_____
_____
_____

If you have questions about whether an item has become an idol in your heart, talk to the Lord about it until you have peace about the way God sees it. If something comes to mind and you are still not sure about whether it is an idol of your heart, write it down with a question mark. Continue praying about the matter until you have some clear direction from the Lord.

If you have identified idols of your heart, pray through the following steps and check each one when you finish.

1. Confess to the Lord that you have given your love and attention to these items or activities. Agree with Him that you have sinned.
2. Ask Him to forgive and cleanse you.
3. Ask Him to set you free from your love for these things. Remember the height from which you have fallen. Return to your first love.
4. Pledge to Him your love and desire to please and obey Him.[2]

---

1. Claude King, *Come to the Lord's Table* (Nashville: LifeWay Press, 2006), 50–51.
2. Ibid., 58–59.

# God's Activity Watch List

Read the following suggestions, keeping in mind the people you listed in your circles of influence. Pray and ask God to identify the people on whom He wants you to focus your prayers and attention.

1. Pray and ask God to reveal the people of His choosing—those God wants you to carry a special concern for in prayer and action. Do you have a special concern to see a particular person come to faith in Christ? Assume that this concern is from God and add the person to your circles of influence.

2. As you pray through your circles of influence, identify people for whom you develop a special concern during prayer.

3. Watch for spiritual interest or spiritual hunger in the lives of those for whom you are praying. Do people in your circles of influence show a special interest in spiritual things? Are they asking questions about spiritual matters?

4. As you pray, pay special attention to a person who surfaces in your circles of influence almost unexpectedly—someone who surprises you. Ask the Lord whether He has brought that person to your mind because of His work in his or her life.

5. Pray more intensely for people when you become aware of a special need they have.

This may be God's invitation for you to show His love by meeting the need. Do you know of special needs in the lives of any of those in your circles of influence? Pray and ask God whether He wants you to reach out to these people during their time of need.

6. Pay special attention to those around you when you experience a crisis together. A crisis may give you a special opportunity to share Christ, meet a need, or demonstrate Christ's peace or wisdom. Have you recently faced a significant crisis with anyone?

7. When you experience a broken relationship with another person, pray about how you can seek reconciliation in a way God can use for divine purposes in the person's life. Has anyone sinned against you to whom you can show God's mercy by forgiving him or her?

8. Watch for people who enter your circles of influence through unique or special circumstances. God may want to use you to introduce them to Christ. Did you add anyone to your circles of influence who has come into your world by unusual circumstances?

---

Claude King, *Final Command Action Manual* (Murfreesboro, TN: Final Command Resources, 2001), 42–43.

## Your Most Wanted

Examine your survey forms for circles 2–6. Pray and ask the Lord which people are on His Most Wanted list for you. Begin making them a special matter of prayer. Begin watching for ways God works through you to show love to them or to build deeper relationships with them.

_____
_____
_____
_____
_____
_____
_____
_____
_____
_____
_____
_____

### SURVEY FORM

Name _____

Address _____

City, state, ZIP _____

Home phone _____ Work phone _____

Cell phone _____ Relationship _____

     ○ Single   ○ Married   ○ Divorced   ○ Widowed   ○ Separated

Prayer requests/needs/circumstances _____

_____

Birthday _____ Anniversary _____

Occupation/place of employment _____

Hobbies/interests _____

Times of joy or stress to remember and date _____

Strategy _____

Date gospel presented _____

Response _____

_____

# Introducing Jesus Christ

After you've prepared your story of what Jesus Christ has done in your life, you can be Christ's witness to the world. Combine your personal testimony with a tool that clearly presents the good news of Jesus Christ and explains how a person can place his or her trust in Christ's promise of salvation.

## WITNESSING TOOLS

1. Gospel tracts like *Eternal Life Witnessing Booklet, Steps to Peace with God,* or *How to Have a Full and Meaningful Life*
2. Marked New Testaments like *Share Jesus Without Fear New Testament* and *Here's Hope New Testament*
3. Christian videos like *Jesus (www.jesusfilm. org),* World Wide Pictures produced by the Billy Graham Evangelistic Association, or *3:16 The Church Experience* by Max Lucado.
4. Evangelism courses like *FAITH Evangelism, Share Jesus Without Fear,* or *Learning to Share My Faith*
5. Sunday School or outreach Bible-study resources *(www.serendipityhouse.com)*

## USING THE TOOLS

The following are nonthreatening ways to use the previously described witnessing tools to share the gospel with those in your circles of influence.

1. *Live testimony.* Share your personal testimony. Leave a tract, New Testament, book, or video and say something like this: "Jesus Christ has made such a difference in my life that I'd like for you to meet Him too."
2. *Lighthouses of Prayer.* Many people pray for their neighbors through Lighthouses of Prayer. After you have taken actions for prayer and care, use your personal testimony and other tools to begin the SHARE phase of your outreach to your neighborhood.
3. *Movie night.* Invite people for whom you are praying in your circles of influence to your home for a movie or video. Share a brief testimony about what Jesus means to you and how the movie has been meaningful to you.
4. *Christmas or Easter letter.* Write a Christmas or Easter letter to family and friends introducing Jesus as the reason for the season. Include your personal testimony.
5. *Church Christmas and Easter presentations.* Invite people to a special presentation or service at your church around Christmas or Easter.
6. *Prayer center.* Set up a table or booth at local festivals, at sports events, at parades, at special events, or in places with large crowds of people like bus stops and transit stations. Ask people how you may pray for them and pray. After praying for people's needs, talk about their relationship with Jesus Christ.
7. *Support-group evangelism.* Provide Christ-centered support groups to minister to people who are trapped in addiction or other needs that can be helped by group support. Help participants realize what Jesus can do for them.

Claude King, *Made to Count Life Planner* (Nashville: LifeWay Press, 2004), 204–5.

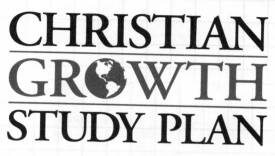

# CHRISTIAN GROWTH STUDY PLAN

In the Christian Growth Study Plan, *Witness to the World* is a resource for course credit in the subject areas Evangelism and Discipleship in the Christian Growth category of diploma plans. To receive credit, read the book; complete the learning activities; attend group sessions; show your work to your pastor, a staff member, or a church leader; then complete the form. This page may be duplicated. Send the completed form to:

**Christian Growth Study Plan: One LifeWay Plaza; Nashville, TN 37234-0117; fax (615) 251-5067; e-mail *cgspnet@lifeway.com***

For information about the Christian Growth Study Plan, refer to the current *Christian Growth Study Plan Catalog*, located online at *www.lifeway.com/cgsp*. If you do not have access to the Internet, contact the Christian Growth Study Plan office, (800) 968-5519, for the specific plan you need.

### *Witness to the World*
### COURSE NUMBER: CG–1258

## PARTICIPANT INFORMATION

Social Security Number (USA ONLY-optional)  — — 

Personal CGSP Number* — 

Date of Birth (MONTH, DAY, YEAR) — — 

Name (First, Middle, Last)

Home Phone — — 

Address (Street, Route, or P.O. Box)

City, State, or Province

Zip/Postal Code

Email Address for CGSP use

Please check appropriate box: ❑ Resource purchased by church ❑ Resource purchased by self ❑ Other

## CHURCH INFORMATION

Church Name

Address (Street, Route, or P.O. Box)

City, State, or Province

Zip/Postal Code

## CHANGE REQUEST ONLY

❑ Former Name

❑ Former Address

City, State, or Province

Zip/Postal Code

❑ Former Church

City, State, or Province

Zip/Postal Code

Signature of Pastor, Conference Leader, or Other Church Leader

Date

*New participants are requested but not required to give SS# and date of birth. Existing participants, please give CGSP# when using SS# for the first time. Thereafter, only one ID# is required. **Mail to:** Christian Growth Study Plan, One LifeWay Plaza, Nashville, TN 37234-0117. Fax: (615)251-5067.

Revised 4-05

# The Growing Disciples Series

New and growing believers need a firm foundation on which to build their lives. The Growing Disciples Series provides short-term Bible studies that establish a strong foundation for a life of following Jesus Christ. The series begins with *The Call to Follow Christ*, which introduces six spiritual disciplines. Subsequent studies help believers understand and practice disciplines that strengthen their love relationship with Christ and develop a lifestyle of faithful, fruitful obedience. Watch for the following six-week resources as the series grows:

Growing Disciples: Abide in Christ
Growing Disciples: Live in the Word
Growing Disciples: Pray in Faith
Growing Disciples: Fellowship with Believers
Growing Disciples: Witness to the World
Growing Disciples: Minister to Others

*The Call to Follow Christ: Six Disciplines for New and Growing Believers* by Claude King is a seven-session, foundational resource that introduces the six disciplines in the series. This unique workbook includes a music CD with seven songs sung by Dámaris Carbaugh that will enrich participants' daily 10- to 15-minute interactive devotion/study time.

Item 001303666

To order these resources and to check availability, fax (615) 251-5933; phone toll free (800) 458-2772; order online at *www.lifeway.com;* e-mail *orderentry@lifeway.com;* visit the LifeWay Christian Store serving you; or write to LifeWay Church Resources Customer Service; One LifeWay Plaza; Nashville, TN 37234-0113.

## Acts 1:8, KJV

"Ye shall receive power, after that the Holy Ghost
is come upon you: and ye shall be witnesses unto me
both in Jerusalem, and in all Judaea, and in Samaria,
and unto the uttermost part of the earth."

## Acts 1:8, HCSB

"You will receive power when the Holy Spirit
has come upon you, and you will be My
witnesses in Jerusalem, in all Judea and
Samaria, and to the ends of the earth."

## Matthew 5:23-24, KJV

"If thou bring thy gift to the altar, and there
rememberest that thy brother hath ought against thee;
Leave there thy gift before the altar, and go
thy way; first be reconciled to thy brother, and
then come and offer thy gift."

## Matthew 5:23-24, HCSB

"If you are offering your gift on the altar, and there
you remember that your brother has something
against you, leave your gift there in front of the
altar. First go and be reconciled with your
brother, and then come and offer your gift."

## John 7:38, KJV

"He that believeth on me, as the scripture
hath said, out of his belly shall flow
rivers of living water."

## John 7:38, HCSB

"The one who believes in Me, as the
Scripture has said, will have streams of
living water flow from deep within him."

## John 15:12, KJV

"This is my commandment, That ye
love one another, as I have loved you."

## John 15:12, HCSB

"This is My command: love
one another as I have loved you."

## 1 Corinthians 9:22, KJV

"I am made all things to all men,
that I might by all means save some."

## 1 Corinthians 9:22, HCSB

"I have become all things to all people,
so that I may by all means save some."

## Matthew 28:18-20, KJV

"All power is given unto me in heaven and in earth. Go ye therefore, and teach all nations, baptizing them in the name of the
Father, and of the Son, and of the Holy Ghost: Teaching them
to observe all things whatsoever I have commanded you: and,
lo, I am with you alway, even unto the end of the world. Amen."

## Matthew 28:18-20, HCSB

"All authority has been given to Me in heaven and on earth. Go,
therefore, and make disciples of all nations, baptizing them in
the name of the Father and of the Son and of the Holy Spirit,
teaching them to observe everything I have commanded you.
And remember, I am with you always, to the end of the age."

*Witness to the World, Week 1*
**Acts 1:8**, HCSB

*Witness to the World, Week 1*
**Acts 1:8**, KJV

*Witness to the World, Week 2*
**Matthew 5:23-24**, HCSB

*Witness to the World, Week 2*
**Matthew 5:23-24**, KJV

*Witness to the World, Week 3*
**John 7:38**, HCSB

*Witness to the World, Week 3*
**John 7:38**, KJV

*Witness to the World, Week 4*
**John 15:12**, HCSB

*Witness to the World, Week 4*
**John 15:12**, KJV

*Witness to the World, Week 5*
**1 Corinthians 9:22**, HCSB

*Witness to the World, Week 5*
**1 Corinthians 9:22**, KJV

*Witness to the World, Week 6*
**Matthew 28:18-20**, HCSB

*Witness to the World, Week 6*
**Matthew 28:18-20**, KJV